T0295770

Music Artist Managers

To what extent is it possible to do good work in music artist management? Drawing upon original research, this shortform book explores and evaluates motivation, remuneration and equity stakes within the music industries.

The author ponders the apparent managerial exodus from the music industries and whether this brain drain could be addressed by providing better remuneration via equity. Based on evidence from Australia, the book illuminates how pay in this sector has remained flat despite increasing responsibility.

Emphasising the quality of the subjective experience of music artist managers, this concise book provides readers with new insights into the important role managers play in the music business. The result is a book that will be useful reading for academics and reflective practitioners.

Guy Morrow is Senior Lecturer in Arts and Cultural Management at the University of Melbourne, Australia.

Routledge Focus on the Global Creative Economy

Series Editor: Aleksandar Brkić

Goldsmiths, University of London, UK

This innovative Shortform book series aims to provoke and inspire new ways of thinking, new interpretations, emerging research, and insights from different fields. In rethinking the relationship of creative economies and societies beyond the traditional frameworks, the series is intentionally inclusive. Featuring diverse voices from around the world, books in the series bridge scholarship and practice across arts and cultural management, the creative industries and the global creative economy.

Creative Work Beyond Precarity
Learning to Work Together
Tim Butcher

Youth Culture and the Music Industry in Contemporary Cambodia
Questioning Tradition
Darathtey Din

Global Crisis and the Creative Industries
Analysing the Impact of the Covid-19 Pandemic
Ryan Daniel

Creative Economy and Sustainable Development
The Context of Indian Handicrafts
Madhura Dutta

Music Artist Managers
Remuneration and Retention in the Popular Music Business
Guy Morrow

For more information about this series, please visit: *www.routledge.com/Routledge-Focus-on-the-Global-Creative-Economy/book-series/RFGCE*

Music Artist Managers

Remuneration and Retention
in the Popular Music Business

Guy Morrow

LONDON AND NEW YORK

First published 2025
by Routledge
4 Park Square, Milton Park, Abingdon, Oxon OX14 4RN

and by Routledge
605 Third Avenue, New York, NY 10158

Routledge is an imprint of the Taylor & Francis Group, an informa business

© 2025 Guy Morrow

The right of Guy Morrow to be identified as author of this work has been asserted in accordance with sections 77 and 78 of the Copyright, Designs and Patents Act 1988.

All rights reserved. No part of this book may be reprinted or reproduced or utilised in any form or by any electronic, mechanical, or other means, now known or hereafter invented, including photocopying and recording, or in any information storage or retrieval system, without permission in writing from the publishers.

Trademark notice: Product or corporate names may be trademarks or registered trademarks, and are used only for identification and explanation without intent to infringe.

British Library Cataloguing-in-Publication Data
A catalogue record for this book is available from the British Library

ISBN: 978-1-032-48227-9 (hbk)
ISBN: 978-1-032-48230-9 (pbk)
ISBN: 978-1-003-38800-5 (ebk)

DOI: 10.4324/9781003388005

Typeset in Times New Roman
by Apex CoVantage, LLC

In loving memory of Michael McMartin 1945–2024

Contents

Preface

In 2022, the Association of Artist Managers (AAM) Australia Chair Greg Carey and Executive Director Maggie Collins approached me to do some research. The AAM is a not-for-profit organisation that is primarily resourced through membership fees. It is part of an international collaborative network of associations that is facilitated by the umbrella organisation the International Music Managers Forum. This invitation, and the setting up of a research contract between the AAM and the University of Melbourne, was the culmination of an idea generated through discussion with former AAM Executive Director Catherine Haridy while she was guest lecturing at my university in 2019.

Related to this project, I was also invited to chair a BIGSOUND panel for the AAM in September 2022 in Brisbane, Australia. The panel was entitled 'Sustainable Relationships? The Value of Management Partnerships'. The premise of this panel discussion was the belief that, even before the COVID-19 pandemic, music artist managers were facing a crisis of career sustainability and that this has been even more challenging since 2020.[1] The panel discussants addressed the questions: What is it about music artist management business structures and modern culture that are driving these challenges? Where do these challenges stem from, and how can music artist managers and their teams overcome them?

I was an obvious choice for this research and associated panel because I researched music artist management within the Australian popular music industries for my PhD, and, following this, I set up my own artist management company and managed and co-managed a number of bands including Boy & Bear, who, under my tenure, achieved platinum album sales in Australia, won five Australian Recording Industry Association awards and achieved international success by selling out shows around the world.

This book will explore the question of whether there is a music artist manager exodus from the music industries and, if there is one, how this 'brain drain' could be addressed. This book was a poignant one for me to research and write because I can be characterised as being part of the exodus of music artist managers from the field caused by the shifting ground beneath music artist manager remuneration. The circumstances or 'contexts' through which music artists build their businesses are changing, yet the terms on which music artists engage managers often have not evolved. Though my past role in the music business and my current position as an educator and researcher employed by the University of Melbourne overlap, I am not necessarily an advocate for managers. The research data collected for this project is what informs this book.

Note

1 **Important note: sensitive themes**

Please note that some of the themes covered in this book may be distressing and include discussion of bullying and self-harm.

In Australia, if you need help you can call the crisis support service Lifeline 13 11 14 or Beyond Blue 1300 224 636.

Acknowledgements

I worked on this book from the unceded lands of the Wurundjeri people of the Kulin nations and on those of the Gadigal people of the Eora Nation and the communities of the GuriNgai and Darug peoples. I pay respect to Elders past, present and future, and acknowledge the importance of Indigenous knowledge in the academy.

Many individuals have assisted and encouraged me throughout my research for this book. In the first instance, I gratefully acknowledge that the research in this book was funded by the Association of Artist Managers (AAM). Thanks to former AAM Executive Director Cath Haridy for initially supporting this idea and current Executive Director Maggie Collins as well as former AAM Chair Greg Carey for finalising the research contract. I also received funding from the University of Melbourne, Faculty of Arts Publishing Support Program. Thank you for making such grants available.

I would also like to thank, in order of appearance, Michael McMartin, Oscar Dawson, John Watson, Keith Welsh, Jess Keeley, David Vodicka, Leigh Treweek and Rowan Brand, as well as all the research participants who wished to remain anonymous, for participating in this project. Thanks also to Annabella Coldrick of the Music Managers' Forum UK and Dr Martin Clancy of AI: OK for meeting with me and sharing ideas.

I would like to thank the following people for their comments on ideas and topics that shaped this book. My colleagues at the University of Melbourne, Dr Brian Long and Dr Kim Goodwin, provided extremely valuable feedback during the final stages of writing this book. Dr Brian Long also worked as a research assistant on the project and copyedited the book. Thanks also to Kate Leeson for additional copyediting work and for providing editorial suggestions, and Kate Adams for your tireless work on behalf of the AAM.

I am also exceptionally grateful to Terry Clague and Naomi Round Cahalin and the rest of the Routledge team who helped birth this book, as well as series editor Aleksandar Brkić.

Thanks to the family and friends who sustain me during my work. While too numerous to name here individually, you know who you are. Thank you so much for supporting me and keeping me going during the researching and writing of this book.

I would like to acknowledge my daughters Zara Yasmin Morrow, Leila Roxana Morrow and Yasmin Parisa Morrow. Yasmin was born during the researching and writing of this book, and I listened to the interview and focus group recordings with her during a long stretch of parental leave in 2023. This greatly assisted my creative process. This book is dedicated to the loving memory of Michael McMartin. Michael was a generous mentor to so many in the field including me and he was interviewed for this book. His quotes rose to the top because he was an unwavering advocate for music artists in a context in which the power of major labels, song publishers, live music promoters and big tech companies has grown. He contributed greatly to the development of a strong and independent artist manager community in Australia, and it is tragic that he passed away before he could read the final version of this book. Hopefully he would have been proud.

Guy Morrow, Melbourne, Victoria
March, 2024

Introduction

The interests and vulnerabilities of music artist managers

Popular music plays a central role in Australian culture and society. It not only provides enjoyment and entertainment, but popular songs can also unite us as a community, help us to understand who we are and inspire us to enact political, social and personal change. These benefits result from the musical and artistic output of music artists. Their commitment is the foundation on which our musical life depends. This book is significant because it addresses concerns about how the music artist managers who support such artists are in turn supported, or not supported, in terms of remuneration, retention, leadership, incentivisation, motivation, reward and ultimately their overall treatment by those who hire them: artists. The core research problem driving this book is: to what extent is it possible for managers to do good, enjoyable and fulfilling work in music artist management? By investigating the quality of the subjective experience of music artist managers, this book lays the foundation for the development of needs-based solutions to some of the issues that music artist managers face.

One significant theme that this book highlights is that, in many instances, music artists need, perhaps counterintuitively, to better lead and manage their managers. While this proposition may initially seem odd, bear with me. First, music artists need to understand that if they have a manager, or want to attract one, they have responsibility for leading, managing, incentivising and motivating them. Second, they need to understand that the other stakeholders surrounding music artists—such as record labels, song publishers and live music promoters—may not be interested in helping to ensure that the management sector is economically sustainable; it is in artists' interests to have strong, independent managers who do not have conflicts of interest because their interests will align with their own. Without experienced managers to help artists leverage better deals, artists risk becoming even more subservient to the chokepoints (Giblin & Doctorow, 2022) that big tech and big content companies use to capture creative labour markets.

Major record labels traditionally, and nowadays also entities like Spotify, YouTube and Live Nation, build monopolies (where sellers have power over

DOI: 10.4324/9781003388005-1

buyers) and monopsonies (where buyers have power over sellers). These monopolies and monopsonies syphon away much of the value that artists create. The key question here is why are the people who have the job of looking out for the best interests of artists themselves on agreements that make them relatively disposable? While artists' lawyers, accountants and booking agents also look out for their interests, these stakeholders usually form a team that is built and led by the manager. Are music artist managers in insecure, vulnerable and increasingly unsustainable positions in the music business because of the behind-the-scenes politicking of major record labels and other powerful entities with whom managers are supposed to negotiate? Or is the situation more benign than this, and are there other reasons for the problems in music artist management? Either way, the position the research participants featured in this book have found themselves in is derivative of how power has historically worked in the music business, as veteran Australian/Canadian artist manager Michael McMartin noted:

> There's an inverse pyramid. Right at the bottom is the creator. Without the creator, there isn't anything to build on. But all of the power, all of the rules, everything starts up here. When you hear the phrase trickle-down economics, that defines how creative arts money flows, the pennies trickle down to the creators. And it's just so obscenely unfair.
>
> .   (Interview 12)

In this book I explore the interests of music artist managers, interests that, for the most part, align with artists' interests, and this is primarily where the significance of this book lies. Strengthening the music artist manager community in Australia has the potential to help more pennies 'trickle down' to the creators, and there are ways to do this without artists handing over more of their finite revenue to their managers. Better leadership and management of managers by artists and governments has the potential to unlock significant cultural and economic value within the music industries overall while simultaneously helping to decentralise and distribute power in these industries. The generative core of these industries pivots on the relationship between artists and their managers. The nucleus of this generative core consists of both artistic creativity and managerial creativity, and I will argue that better systems, structures, cultures and support need to be placed around the latter type of creativity. Doing so will help to address the inequities derived from the fact that this generative core lies at the bottom of the inverted music business pyramid of power.

About this book

In Chapter 1 I set the context for my arguments by introducing the work of music artist managers, their relationships with artists and common characteristics of music artist agreements. To give my arguments a theoretical footing, in Chapter 2 I will turn to ideas about reward management. I will link such writing to leadership research and social psychology. In the organisational and business management literature, reward management comes from attempts to explain employee motivation. The transactions inherent in reward-management processes discussed in the literature mostly occur within firms. In this book, however, I am applying reward management theory to transactions between independent economic agents rather than within a firm. The artist and the manager's businesses are usually separate. A manager typically has several artists on their books while large, internationally operating management companies with a stable of managers enjoy increasing prominence in the music industries. So, the question becomes how one incentivises and leads the other through a contract between two different businesses.

In Chapter 3 I outline the issues and challenges that music artist managers face. This chapter primarily focuses on artist management agreements; these agreements are at the core of many of the problems this book addresses, and negotiation of these agreements is arguably within a manager's circle of control. Chapter 4 outlines the problems stemming from the seemingly ever-expanding role of music artist managers. While managers' pay is often ill-defined, the scope of the work they are required to do often is too. Finally, Chapter 5 presents new models for music artist manager retention.

Theories relating to negative leadership versus motivational leadership then help us to understand both artist-to-manager leadership and manager-to-artist leadership in this context. I specifically use ideas concerning the relative effects of different leadership variables on creativity and innovation because this book focuses on the motivation of music artist managers themselves to create and innovate in their roles. I then use self-determination theory (SDT) (Deci & Ryan, 2012) to explain this motivation and to present a framework for needs-supportive artist-to-manager leadership that encompasses both financial and non-financial rewards. According to SDT, autonomy, relatedness and competence are three universal psychological needs that are essential for optimal human development and functioning. The theory is used to explain non-financial reward management among music artist managers. Combined, these theories explain both financial and non-financial reward management. This matters because managers play a role in building and maintaining commercial music ecosystems; the incentivisation and motivation of managers is crucial to the flourishing of these ecosystems.

How this research was conducted

To investigate these drivers among managers, I used a multi-method approach (Tashakkori & Teddlie, 1998) that included a survey, interviews and focus groups. The participants included music artist managers, music artists and music lawyers who work in the music industries. When selecting participants, I tried to achieve a balance between the number of men and women participating. Balance was also sought in terms of the following dimensions: length of experience, age of the participants and managers working for larger artist management companies and those working on a freelance basis. Recruitment was facilitated by the Association of Artist Managers (AAM).

All members (population N = 278) of the AAM were invited to complete the survey questionnaire in 2022. Seventy-seven AAM members completed the questionnaire. Quantitative survey data was collected via Qualtrics and analysed using SPSS. The free-text short answers were analysed with the support of NVivo. Thematic analysis, a process of identifying patterns or themes within qualitative data, was then conducted. The survey generated quantitative data and relatively short free-text responses. This survey was then followed by methods that allowed more in-depth exploration of the themes. These included interviews and focus groups that picked up on the key themes raised by the survey. Following the 2022 survey, in 2023, I interviewed 17 participants and conducted two focus groups. The interviews and focus groups enabled me to engage with the participants in often-lengthy discussions of the key issues.

In summary, to understand the complex functioning of music artist management as a cog at the centre of the music industries, we need to grasp the essence of serious and professional music artist management practice—how managers allocate their time and earn money, what factors support or inhibit the achievement of their goals and those of their clients, how their working conditions are changing and in what ways factors such as management agreements may need to change and evolve to reflect these changes. Further, when considering the question of why music artist managers do this type of work in the first place— what is good and fulfilling about the work—there emerged a sense that many perennial elements remain. Managers are intrinsically motivated. They love music and helping their clients pursue artistic visions. Managers' role in helping to connect these visions with audiences can bring them immense joy. These incentives remain at the heart of why many music artist managers continue in the role. But for increasing numbers of them, keeping a grip on these core values in a rapidly changing business is proving more difficult than ever. We need to accord music artist managers the respect they deserve as professionals who dedicate their skills to enriching our culture. There is a pressing need to revisit and reassess the incentives that motivate managers to continue managing.

References

Deci, E. L., & Ryan, R. M. (2012). Self-determination theory. In P. A. M. Van Lange, A. W. Kruglanski, & E. T. Higgins (Eds.), *Handbook of theories of social psychology: Volume 1* (pp. 416–437). SAGE. https://doi.org/10.4135/9781446249215

Giblin, R., & Doctorow, C. (2022). *Chokepoint capitalism: How big tech and big content captured creative labor markets and how we'll win them back.* Scribe Publications.

Tashakkori, A., & Teddlie, C. (1998). *Mixed methodology: Combining qualitative and quantitative approaches.* SAGE.

1 What is music artist management?

The role of the music artist manager

When it comes to defining music artist management, metaphors and analogies abound. Many of these are useful here. They include picturing the artist or band as a board of directors, and the manager as the chief executive officer (CEO) (AAM, 2022); visualising the artist as being like a tree and the manager the roots (AAM, 2022); explaining that the artist and manager relationship forms the hub of a bicycle wheel with the other stakeholders forming the spokes (Watson, 2002); visualising the manager as the opposite side of the yin-yang symbol from the artist; picturing the manager as a punching bag or a shock absorber; and the manager conceptualised as the driver of the artist's truck as it hurtles down a highway.[1] Before further explaining these metaphors and analogies, it is worth linking them to the discussion of incentivisation in the introduction by asking: Are managers incentivised as CEOs are? Is enough water being poured on the roots? Is the relationship at the hub of the wheel sustainable? Does the yin-yang symbol depict a healthy relationship? Is it OK to be treated as a punching bag? Is the driver of the truck so overworked that they are falling asleep at the wheel?

According to the AAM, managers often respond to these questions with a 'no'—apart from the last question to which the answer is 'yes', managers often endure such overwork that they fall asleep at the wheel. This is why in 2022 the AAM signed up to the Australian Contemporary Music Industry's joint submission to the Australian government's renewed National Cultural Policy consultation. The AAM opened its contribution by defining music artist management using a clear CEO analogy: the manager is a specialist in each music artist's career strategy and is responsible for executing this strategy in consultation with the board, with a view to mobilising the other stakeholders who are engaged on a contract or freelance basis (i.e., the booking agent, the record label, the song publisher, etc.) (see AAM, 2022). Concerningly though, later in the submission the analogy used became that of a business partnership

DOI: 10.4324/9781003388005-2

with one partner being at times problematically subservient to the other to the point of them being bullied:

> The most obvious comparison for the artist/manager relationship would be that of a business partnership where one party is the Creative Director, and the other is the CEO. But there is one stark difference. Despite the manager often being the one with the most expertise on the industry, they are intrinsically subservient to the artist.[2] This immediately creates a complex power imbalance, and is a recipe for friction, disagreements and even,—contrary to Hollywood's outdated depiction of Managers as the 'villain'—artist-to-manager bullying.
>
> (Association of Artist Managers, 2022)

Power and bullying in the artist-manager relationship

The artist-manager relationship is complex. The potential power imbalance mentioned here may only arise later in the relationship because the balance of power tends to shift as success[3] accumulates:

> A rise in the level of success will see the power balance shift in the artist's favour. However, in the period before success and after a decline in success the power balance will be in the artist manager's favour. This power balance is constantly evolving and differs across genres.
>
> (Morrow, 2006, p. 4)

Concerningly, instances of artist-to-manager bullying that may occur when the power balance shifts in the artist's favour are difficult for managers to address for several reasons. First, the artist may not conceptualise their relationship with their manager as an employer-employee or contractor one because they think of themself as an 'artist', not a 'businessperson', a conceptualisation informed by the romantic notion of a separation between art and commerce (Bilton, 2006; Negus, 1996). Second, such instances are also difficult to address because a music artist manager can be thought of as 'a person who earns a living from helping artists build and maximise their musical careers' (Watson, 2002, p. 2), and because 'a manager's job is to create the perception that the band is successful' (Woodruff, 2002, as cited in Morrow, 2006, p. 59). Therefore, disclosing a client's poor behaviour towards a manager risks undermining the perception of success the manager wants to create. One research participant, who is a senior Australian artist manager, recalled attending a meeting with other senior managers at which the managers discussed

> artists taking out their frustrations and their own intense mental health issues on their managers, and these managers, who only have one or two clients

that are paying the bills, feel like 'I kind of gotta cop it'. And I was thinking how interesting it was, in a world where so much of the discourse around bullying is about the bullying of artists—and there's been a lot of that, and it needs to stop, and the efforts in that direction are to be applauded—there's also been an awful lot of bullying in [record] labels, that's been much discussed too, the efforts to stop that are to be applauded and, hopefully, the future will be much better. But listening to this conversation around this table, I think there's actually a lot of bullying happening from artists to managers. Which nobody could ever say. The manager would feel like they were being a wuss to admit to something like that. It would also make their artists look really bad, and that's bad for the business. The manager will excuse it away, in the way that people do in enabling relationships, by saying 'Well, you know, they've got mental health struggles. They were just upset.' You know, 'It's Monday morning. He won't do it to me next weekend.' I came away from it feeling like there were a lot of those people who were in really abusive relationships. And it really surprised me. The core of it was . . . the people who were talking about it and getting teary about it were people who really depended upon that client to put a roof over their head. They were the ones getting phone calls at 3 am.

(Interview 17)

Of course, not all artist-manager relationships are abusive—each is unique—and as indicated in this quotation, there are examples of manager-to-artist bullying. Further, in contrast to the artist-to-manager bullying example mentioned earlier, the participant who provided this example continued by saying: 'A smart artist—certainly the smart artists I work with—they're smart enough to recognise that it's good for their business to motivate their manager, just like a good board of directors motivates their CEO' (Interview 17). However, to understand why some managers stay in abusive relationships with their clients, and to define what music artist management is more clearly, how managers go about their work and how secure they feel in their roles, it is useful here to outline the typical remuneration structures that are used, enshrined in artist management agreements.

Artist management agreements

Remuneration structures and systems are influenced by the context and culture in which they are implemented and the power relations that exist between employers and employees (Druker & White, 2009). Music artist managers typically work with artists on a relatively insecure basis. The management agreements that were discussed by my research participants are service provision agreements. These agreements typically begin with a trial period of three to six months, after which many agreements continue on a rolling basis until one of the parties gives 30 to 60 days' written notice that they want to terminate the agreement, while other agreements are for a set term of up to five years. The manager's services are not exclusive to the artist, though the artist is usually exclusively managed by the manager or management firm with the world as the territory. In the typical agreement, the manager does not acquire copyright in any material the artist owns or controls (usually musical works, lyrics or arrangements). A manager usually receives a commission of between 15 and 25 per cent of the artists' adjusted gross or net income

- paid as a result of the artist's studio and live recording endeavours (including motion picture, television or video performances),
- from any songwriting endeavours or composer services, and
- from merchandise if exploited by a third party or less expenses if the artist exploits their merchandise on their own.

The commission from live performance income is often a point of tension between music artists, their lawyers and music artist managers. At the heart of such discussions lie questions about what is deducted from gross income before the manager's commission is calculated. Some savvy lawyers engaged by managers negotiate for net touring income to be the gross income from live performances after the deduction of booking agent and support act fees, all advertising and promotion expenses directly associated with the relevant live performance and all direct venue costs and live production expenses (including venue hire, equipment, lighting and PA hire). Artists and their lawyers, on the other hand, sometimes seek to deduct travel and accommodation costs and the daily per diems paid to artists while they are on tour in their definitions of 'net touring income'. The deduction of these latter expenses is 'net' from the perspective of the music artist. Negotiations concerning what is included or excluded as deductions from live performance income will dramatically increase or decrease the manager's commission because live performance income is the main source of income for music artists (see Tschmuck, 2017, p. 125) and therefore also for music artist managers.

Another source of tension concerns post-term commissions. Typically, as outlined earlier, managers are incentivised by the promise of deferred compensation by way of commissions on income that derives from work they did while under contract. If their management agreement lacks a provision for post-term commissions that will endure for long enough to reflect their investment of time and it is terminated on the eve of an album release, a large tour they have helped put together or some other project, they may not receive an appropriate share of the income that comes in after their contract ends. These post-term commission rates range from 100 per cent of the manager's commission for the first year following termination, down to 75, 50 or 25 per cent for each of the following years, or whatever is agreed. The survey results, interviews and focus groups indicated that, typically, the post-termination commission rate tapers down over a period of between three to five years.

However, in the age of music streaming—when revenue from recorded music has a much longer tail than it did in previous eras—some managers and lawyers I interviewed argued that there are grounds for a longer and slower tapering post-term period that includes 5 per cent of the original commission rate (or often 20 per cent) in perpetuity. Arguments concerning such participation in the revenue generated by assets that were created during the manager's term, including perpetual commissions, also involve managers arguing that they bring a 'talent' to the business; it was partly their managerial creativity (Morrow, 2006) during the term of their agreement that helped to achieve such long-term results.

So why do typical management agreements lead to managers having feelings of insecurity, anxiety and fear? Basically, if an artist does not want a manager to manage them anymore, there is not much a manager can do about it. According to one senior Australian-Canadian manager I interviewed, Michael McMartin:

> One of the negatives is that you can have all the contracts in the world, but if an artist says that's the end of the day, that's the end of it, the contract is not worth anything. So that is always a worry for most managers. The upside is you will probably see it coming before the artist does.
>
> (Interview 12)

Managers are speculative investors of their time, and they are exposed to the high risk that their investment will not see a return by way of deferred compensation if the artist becomes commercially successful. While to an extent this is the nature of entrepreneurship in a field with very high commercial failure rates caused by oversupply and cut-throat competition, the issue is also caused by the nature of management agreements because, unlike other small-business operators, through these agreements managers do not own what they are creating; they do not have equity in the artist's business, and they often have relatively short post-term commission structures in their agreements. One participant noted: 'It's pretty terrifying in this industry even if you do work to longish contracts . . . every manager's pretty twitchy' (Focus Group 1). Another participant in this focus group stated: 'You're the last to get thanked and the first to get fired' (Focus Group 1). Regarding deferred compensation, a different participant in this group explained:

> There's this odd duality of being super paranoid about losing a client. So, you're overworking, you're over-delivering, you're not really setting boundaries, because we're all terrible at it. But at the same time, those artists really aren't paying us anything. So, it's just this strange duty of care mix where you're so entrepreneurial, and you're so driven to build your business, which includes leveraging the work of someone else.
>
> (Focus Group 1)

Managers are in a risky situation under management agreements like those outlined earlier because of their outlay of time and energy on the promise of deferred compensation through agreements that do not provide them with a long-term interest in what they are building. Yet the upside of the risk they take is that

> it's a model where you don't invest financially, and the ceiling is quite high and that's unique in the business world. You invest a lot of time, and you certainly take a lot of risk, but unlike being a label, publisher or even a festival, you don't take the risk of losing a hundreds of thousands of dollars.
>
> (Interview 8)

While this participant was ignoring the opportunity cost a manager incurs, ultimately, the manager's success is largely dependent on the work of someone else—the artist—and this causes anxiety. An interview participant confided:

> For me, that deep underlying anxiety for every manager I know, that sits there, that's always there. It never leaves you. It doesn't matter how long or how deep that relationship [with an artist] is . . . it eats away at you psychologically, and it puts you in a position of disadvantage with an artist pretty much at all times.
>
> (Interview 6)

Part of the problem is the labour-intensive nature of managers' work. The work is so all-consuming that they cannot take on many clients. While some management companies in Australia such as Unified Music Group solve this issue by taking on more staff (including junior managers) to grow their business in a similar way to a doctor who cannot take on more patients and hires another doctor or enters a partnership with another and starts a surgery. Lawyers and accountants do the same. In contrast, in the Australian music industries, music artist managers are most commonly sole traders with a small number of clients. This contrasts, for example, with live music booking agents who typically book more clients because they focus on one area: live performance. Music artist managers are generalists who work across all areas of the music business, and so they typically invest more time in one artist despite the risk of their management agreement being terminated.

Notes

1 One research participant, Australian artist manager John Watson, provided the latter three metaphors and analogies in an interview and explained the last one as follows: 'I always conceptualise three basic types of managers. If you think about your career as being like a truck driving down the highway, some artists just want to party in the back of the truck and let the

manager drive the truck wherever they want to go. That usually ends up with the manager driving the truck over a cliff and absconding with all the money and the artists spending the rest of their life walking around going, "What the hell just happened?" Some artists want to drive the truck themselves, just have the manager be a bull bar on the front, they know exactly where they want to go. They know everything, just get stuff out of the way. That can occasionally work for very experienced or extraordinarily gifted artists that have no weak spots. But, generally speaking, artists will come a cropper in that situation because they don't know what they don't know. And then there's the third type, which is, obviously, how we would conceptualise our role with our clients, which is as a navigator. You sit down and you work out where the artist wants to take their career and you agree on a plan together on what that destination looks like and how you're going to get there. Then you help them navigate their way to that point' (Interview 13).

2 It is worth noting here that this is common to shared leadership arts management models across the performing arts. According to Goodwin (2017), 'Lapierre (2001) argues that the true leadership role will always reside with the artistic leader, relegating others within the organisation to a lesser status' (p. 53).

3 The term 'success' is being used here to refer to both a musician's creative and commercial success.

References

Association of Artist Managers (AAM). (2022). *National cultural policy submission*. www.aam.org.au/cps2022

Bilton, C. (2006). *Management and creativity: From creative industries to creative management*. Wiley-Blackwell.

Druker, J., & White, G. (2009). Introduction. In G. White & J. Druker (Eds.), *Reward management: A critical text* (2nd ed., pp. 1–22). Routledge.

Goodwin, K. (2017). *Cultural leadership in practice: Leadership identity construction in the Australian arts and cultural sector* [Doctoral thesis, University of Technology Sydney]. Opus. https://opus.lib.uts.edu.au/handle/10453/120335

Morrow, G. (2006). *Managerial creativity: A study of artist management practices in the Australian popular music industry* [Doctoral thesis, Macquarie University]. Figshare. https://figshare.mq.edu.au/articles/thesis/Managerial_creativity_a_study_of_artist_management_practices_in_the_Australian_popular_music_industry/19427489

Negus, K. (1996). *Popular music in theory*. Polity Press-Blackwell.

Tschmuck, P. (2017). *The economics of music*. Agenda Publishing.

Watson, J. (2002). What is a manager? In M. McMartin, S. Eliezer, & S. Quintrell (Eds.), *The music manager's manual* (pp. 1–11). Music Manager's Forum.

2 Managers in the music business
A theoretical framework

Introduction

Following Hesmondhalgh and Baker (2011), the research problem I explore is: to what extent is it possible for managers to do good, enjoyable and fulfilling work in music artist management? By answering this question, I seek to emphasise the quality of the subjective experience of music artist managers. What kinds of experiences does the role of artist management in the music industries offer? Can a framework for needs-supportive artist-to-manager leadership address some of the problems managers are experiencing?

Rather than focus on the regulation of music artist management from a legal perspective (see Gilenson, 1990; Hertz, 1988; Krasilovsky & Meloni, 1990; Morrow, 2013; O'Brien, 1992) or further contribute to the 'descriptive' literature that describes music artist managers' roles in strategy development for career success and the way in which the music artist manager coordinates everyone in the team surrounding the musician (Anderton et al., 2013, p. 185; Bilton & Leary, 2002; Frascogna & Hetherington, 2011; Jones, 2012. See also the 'how to be a music artist manager' literature: Allen, 2018; Weiss & Gaffney, 2012), this book focuses on the motivation of music artist managers themselves. I will discuss theories relating to intrinsic motivation, such as self-determination theory. Further, I examine leadership theories relating to both intrinsic and extrinsic motivation to reconsider the typical reward structures that exist for managers. In doing so, I examine managers' motivation both in relation to whether music artist management can be good work, and the extent to which financial and non-financial reward management could be better utilised.

I also address the following research sub-questions: Can more innovative artist management agreements or even shareholder agreements that provide equity in the musicians' business better incentivise music artist managers? Would such agreements better enable artists to motivate, rather than negatively lead, their managers? This book is significant because, for example, it helps address some of the problems, such as short-term thinking on the part

DOI: 10.4324/9781003388005-3

of managers, that Chaparro and Musgrave (2021) identified concerning moral music artist management and ethical decision-making (or lack thereof) and their possible contribution to the tragic suicide of Swedish DJ and composer Avicii. As I will discuss further in Chapter 3, this tragedy brought to light an argument that this artist's manager neglected a key aspect of the management relationship, particularly an allegation that the manager failed to exercise their duty of care.

My approach here is novel because, while there is much more weight placed on the role of the music artist manager within the contemporary and post-digital popular music business ecosystem—and the sustainability of many artists' careers and associated business entities is dependent on this role—the role is one that has been widely stereotyped and negatively depicted in the media (Anderton et al., 2013) and in the literature. One novel contribution of my work here, therefore, is to offer alternative and at times much more positive depictions of the role. This contrasts, for example, with the work of Dannen (1991), who highlighted unethical and abusive practices that were widespread in the early days of the contemporary recording business. Although some, such as I, have tried to challenge negative music artist manager stereotypes in the past (Morrow, 2006; Rogan, 1988), there is a need for a critical and analytical examination of the role of music artist managers within the 'new' music industries (Hughes et al., 2016), as opposed to perpetuating stereotypes from an era when the music business was even more patriarchal than it is now. More recently, Williamson (2016) outlined the need for research that highlights the diversity in this sector, and that includes voices beyond those of the white men who tend to feature prominently in the extant music artist management literature. This book builds on this work.

In the survey I conducted in collaboration with the AAM, representative responses reflecting the challenges music artist managers face included:

No HR [human resource management].

Being a manager has never been harder. I know a lot of managers on the brink of quitting, myself included.

I spoke to another high-profile manager who is quitting this week. He manages one of the biggest acts in the country and he felt comfortable telling me [thoughts of] suicide was one motivation. It's pretty crazy times.

(Survey)

These responses highlight that many managers feel that they suffer from a lack of support while working in a role that has become harder. This lack of support is leading them to quit due to their deteriorating mental health. In this chapter I therefore apply HR theory to a context in which there is a severe lack of knowledge concerning HR best practices.

Reward management

For Druker and White (2009), reward management has a key position within HR theory and is a discrete area of study. According to Perkins (2019), reward management stands 'at the interdisciplinary interface between economics, industrial relations and HRM, industrial psychology and organizational sociology' (p. 5). In the agreements outlined in Chapter 1, the artist financially rewards the manager. Such rewards are, however, ill-defined because they derive from the artist's financial success. Through a typical agreement the manager could earn 15 to 20 per cent of nothing, or 15 to 20 per cent of a large sum.

In this chapter I distinguish leadership from management. While these terms may sometimes be used interchangeably, leadership and management are actually different from each other, and, in this chapter, I draw out these differences in the hope of both better understanding the manager's role, and developing the notion of artist-to-manager leadership. Delineating artist-to-manager leadership in this context is not a simple task given the many different types of leadership and ways it is defined. There are many different theories from which I could draw, and out of the theories available I chose transactional leadership and transformational leadership.

In a commission-based agreement such as the one outlined in Chapter 1, there is a very clear relationship between performance and reward. The 'performance' here relates to both the artist's and manager's performances in their roles, though the artist's performance is more visible. The manager is rewarded with a share of the amount the artist receives for their combined performance. Artist-to-manager leadership can, therefore, first be characterised as a form of transactional leadership. Transactional leadership involves leaders using extrinsic motivators (rewards or punishments) that are exchanged with their subordinates in transactions designed to achieve optimal job performance. Because a major aspect of this type of leadership is contingent reward, transactional leadership places an emphasis on a clear relationship between performance and reward (Bass & Riggio, 2005).

However, the situation is more nuanced than this. The artist as the leader who financially rewards the manager does not usually specify the manager's reward for work on a specific goal or project. The manager's remuneration is a share of the artist's total earnings as agreed and stipulated in the management agreement. The relationship between performance and reward is agreed in general terms at the outset of the artist—manager collaboration, rather than in each instance of the performance of a specific project. Any payment subject to the management agreement is also deferred. The manager does the work upfront and then receives a commission if the artist generates revenue from their combined efforts. In this sense, the artist's leadership is 'deferred transactional' leadership. Further, transactional leadership is a style of leadership that arguably devalues the relationship between the leader and the subordinate, and it is therefore unlikely to bring out the best in the manager. This is a weakness of transactional approaches.

Artist-to-manager leadership can, therefore, also be described as transformational; these styles of leadership complement each other, and artists do both. Transformational leadership involves the promise of transformation through the leader's actions and the way a leader can motivate teams or followers to think beyond their immediate self-interests. Transformational leaders achieve this by creating a vision of how to achieve the desired change. Both parties, the leader and the follower(s), are transformed/changed through the process which involves improvement and growth. This is an important process of leadership here because, while managers are motivated by the potential of a financial reward, this motivation is accompanied by substantial risk in terms of their time and efforts. The risks are often much higher when managing emerging artists. Antoni (2019) noted that 'transformational leaders communicate an attractive vision, provide meaning, and respond to an employee's values, needs, and goals' (p. 21). However, artists are arguably reluctant leaders (Goodwin, 2020) or may not even be aware that they have a leadership role in relation to their manager because the reward system is established through the management agreement at the outset of the relationship and may not, then, be revisited unless there is a problem. Further, experience in the music business is also relevant here. Emerging artists who sign a management deal with some of the managers I interviewed, who have 30 or more years' experience, might struggle to see themselves as 'leading' such a manager. While it may seem counterintuitive to argue that artists lead their managers, and in other ways managers lead artists, acknowledging this is a key solution to several problems that my research identified.

Transformational leadership theory is useful here because the manager is motivated to help the artist create and may derive benefit from the inherent vision and meaning such artistic creativity can bring. In this chapter I argue that managers are willing to invest their time because they are searching for a promised connection and sense of belonging to a broader community and their artists. As the interview and focus group data I provide later indicates, this proximity to the creative process can help managers feel meaningfully involved with artistic and social communities they value.

This forms part of the psychological contract to which managers implicitly agree. There are explicit terms outlined in the management agreement, as described in Chapter 1. Then there are also implicit, unwritten and intangible non-financial agreements or understandings at play. The psychological contract between an artist and their manager is an unwritten, intangible contract that involves more than the rewards in the mix. It also concerns expectations, understandings and informal commitments, and it fills the gaps left by the narrow and reductive outline of the relationship in the written management agreement or contract.

In this chapter I shed light on this psychological contract, because how both parties understand—or do not understand—their relationship beyond the terms of the written agreement outlined in Chapter 1 is key to their motivation. Antoni (2019) noted that 'research has shown the key role of leadership behaviour for the development and fulfilment or breach of psychological contracts, and consequently for the effects of reward management systems' (p. 22). In this chapter I argue that a key solution to some of the problems articulated by managers would be artists better understanding that they have a leadership role and adopting best practices in this leadership role.

Trust, pay satisfaction and needs support are all themes addressed in this chapter. A trust-based relationship is needed for managers to accept pay that is based on risk. As I will outline later, needs support that addresses the three psychological needs of relatedness, competence and autonomy trumps pay satisfaction to a certain degree. It is not that artists are deliberately adopting non-financial methods to motivate their managers. Instead, non-financial rewards are embedded in the role by default due to its link to creativity and to the artist's creative process.

The concept of total reward is, therefore, useful. Armstrong and Murlis (2007) explained the total reward approach in the following way:

> The total reward concept emphasises the importance of all aspects of the rewards package as a coherent whole . . . account is taken of all the ways in which people can be rewarded and obtain satisfaction through their work, linking financial and non-financial aspects.
>
> (As cited in Brown, 2019, p. 59)

The total reward concept is obviously relevant for emerging artists at the outset of an artist-manager relationship because the contingent reward takes the form of a commission on the revenue that may or may not be generated by the artist's enterprise. This commission can be low for early-career artists, and in this phase non-financial rewards can be important for the manager. Interestingly, such rewards also remain relevant for established artist-manager relationships. Regarding artist management agreements, senior Australian-Canadian artist manager Michael McMartin noted:

> They're appropriate as a guide. And that's all they are, is a guide. My personal agreement with the Hoodoo Gurus over 40 years, it's changed at least five times where you go, 'Okay, look, I'm going to cut this out', where they go, 'We don't want you to share in that anymore.' And going, 'Okay, well, here's the follow-on effect of that.' You work out what's acceptable, and what's not on the presumption that your first agreement is the best agreement you'll ever get. And after that it's Band-Aid fixing. There's negotiation on either side. And I think that's a really good thing because you're constantly reminding yourself and the artist of the value

of management. And it may not be as valuable as you thought, in certain areas, and may be more valuable than the artists thought in others. So, to me, a service agreement is a living document that should be open to discussion and to change and negotiation.

(Interview 12)

In this instance, the financial reward was steadily reduced over a forty-year period through consistent renegotiation of the management agreement. While the longevity of this relationship does offer hope for the sustainability of artist-manager relationships generally, the fact that the financial reward decreased over time, but the relationship remained intact, is interesting. It suggests that consistently increasing financial rewards is not typically used by artists to motivate their managers, quite the opposite. McMartin continued: 'I'm not really aware of many circumstances where the artist has gone, "You're right, you know, you're doing a great job, you deserve so much more." I've not really come across that circumstance before' (Interview 12).

Such renegotiations may involve the artist reducing the manager's compensation as their pot of revenue grows by shifting to a fee-for-service or a salary-based agreement rather than a commission-based one. They may be able to do this because they are commercially successful enough to have the leverage to do so. However, such renegotiation may, at other times, simply reflect the life cycle of a band such as the Hoodoo Gurus; the band may generate different amounts of revenue from various sources compared to earlier phases of their career.

Nevertheless, the negotiation and renegotiation of the management agreement is a delicate balance, and some artists do articulate the way in which they use financial rewards to motivate their manager. For example, one high-profile Australian music artist who participated in a panel the AAM produced and that I chaired for the BIGSOUND festival and conference in 2022, Oscar Dawson,[1] clearly understood the role artists need to play in motivating the managers they employ: 'As an artist . . . I want to make them money, so they keep working' (Dawson et al., 2022). Dawson is aware of his role as a transactional leader here.

Record producer agreements

Another element relating to reward management for music artist managers that needs to be factored into artist-to-manager leadership is a social comparison process across roles in the music business. A particularly sore point for managers concerns the differences between their artist management agreements and the agreements artists may form with a record producer, for example. In contrast to the types of management agreements outlined in Chapter 1, producers are often paid an initial fee and royalties. The term 'points' refers to a percentage of the total royalties. For example, a royalty share of 15 per cent of net income assigned to the producer in perpetuity would be 15 points. This royalty is usually payable following recoupment of the recording costs.

Typically, if the artist is independent, they retain ownership of all copyright both in the master recording and in any musical or literary works embodied on the master recording. If there is a record label involved, then the label may own or licence the master recordings depending on the type of agreement in place, and the producer would still be paid a royalty without owning the intellectual property. Antoni (2019) noted that 'the social comparison process between one's own input and reward, and another person's input and reward relationship, is explained by equity and organizational justice theories' (p. 17). These theories specifically concern distributive justice. The managers I interviewed argued that they work more hours than record producers, but their management agreements are less favourable to them than producer agreements, and therefore they feel that distributive justice is absent. An example of this social comparison process at play in the music business and the alleged lack of distributive justice is encapsulated in the following quotation from Australian artist manager John Watson:

> There are artists I managed whose songs have made millions of dollars in sync licensing[2] in the years since my trailing commissions stopped existing. I'm fine with that. It was the deal I did. I have no resentment towards it. But it is a reality that the reason why those songs continue to resonate in the sync world is because of all the work that a whole bunch of people did. The band first and foremost, but also their record company, their then publisher, and myself, at the time, 15 years ago, in establishing those songs in a whole heap of big movies and that continues to put them top-of-mind for music supervisors. The record company continues to take their piece of it, the producer continues to take their piece of it, on these masters, but the manager does not. I'm not complaining for myself, that's the deal that I did. But if that was the only success I had ever had, then I probably would feel bitter. . . . I've had plenty of other things that have put braces on my kids' teeth, that's not an issue. But I can see if that was your one rodeo, then of course you'd be upset about it.
>
> (Interview 13)

An issue stemming from this for music artist manager retention in the music business is that managers may simply decide to look for another job when they notice that colleagues get paid more and/or enjoy more secure and longer-term rewards for comparable work.

The difference between leadership and management

One aspect of transformational leadership is creating an environment in which others can realise their potential (Bass & Riggio, 2005; Bennis, 2009; Catmull, 2014; Kotter, 2000). As per the CEO analogy outlined in Chapter 1, music artist managers are certainly leaders in this sense; their role involves creating an environment in which their clients can realise their potential. However, as outlined earlier, this also applies in the reverse; artists lead their managers or management teams, and thus their role involves creating an environment in which their managers can realise their potential. Both music artist management and working as an artist involve leadership which, as I will explain later, can be defined differently to management. The consensus from the managers who participated in the survey, focus groups and interviews I conducted was that artist management agreements, as they stand, often do not lead to the creation and maintenance of an environment in which managers can realise their potential. While the psychological contract between an artist and manager may help to pick up the slack here, this has consequences for the management and leadership they can provide, which can in turn affect the interests of artists as well as the broader music business ecology. One interview participant noted that the deep underlying anxiety caused by typical artist management agreements was

> part of the reason why sometimes, and I certainly would not include myself in this, but I know it's happened with others on many occasions, that decisions are made, or recommendations are given to artists based on that fear. Agreeing with an artist for the sake of agreeing with an artist might not be the right decision to make. Saying no, that's not a good idea [is sometimes important]. Artist managers will pull back on actually making those calls because of that underlying anxiety and that fear of losing [their client] . . . artists aren't getting that more objective advice, or just the advice they perhaps even think they're getting. The power dynamic that we talked about, which is integral, it's always out of whack. It's always with the artist. . . . And that's because of the way that agreements are structured. . . . [They're not] fit for purpose reflections of the work that is undertaken.
>
> (Interview 6)

This manager did not believe that management agreements like those outlined in Chapter 1 were secure enough for them to be able to provide appropriate leadership due to a lack of trust in the relationship. In this context, leadership and management are not the same. Leadership should be exercised in a more proactive way than the more reactive strategies of management. Leadership involves 'inspiring' change and the people involved in the realisation of a proactive strategy, whereas, in contrast, managers are often trying to establish stability of some sort and 'manage' people more than inspire them. For Kotter (2001), there are clear differences between management and leadership: 'Management is about coping with complexity. Leadership, by contrast, is about coping with change.' According to him, leadership involves establishing direction—developing a vision and strategies to achieve it—whereas management involves planning, budgeting and organising staffing—the detailed steps and timetables required to achieve a plan. In terms of outcomes, leaders produce change, managers produce predictability and order (Kotter, 2000, 2001).

My research participants indicated that music artist management has most certainly involved coping with change in recent times, both for them personally and helping artists cope with change, which is where leadership comes in. Given that the CEO analogy outlined in Chapter 1 was often used in the interviews, managers do consider themselves to be leaders. But what is the balance between leadership and management? Should the role be thought of as 'music artist leader' and their work as 'music artist leadership'? Or do artists lead, and managers manage, with the artist leading the manager? Does the artist lead the manager in terms of artistic creativity and vision and the manager lead the artist in terms of managerial creativity (see Morrow, 2018, pp. 8–9) and innovation and execution of the vision? Both the artist and manager roles involve leadership, and therefore it is shared between the roles and alternates between them. For Kotter (2001), management and leadership are different but complementary, and in a context of rapid and constant change, one cannot function without the other.

One of the complications, though, and one of the reasons why Kotter's (2001) work is not directly applicable to music artist management, is that, in his words, the practices and procedures of 'management' 'are largely a response to one of the most significant developments of the twentieth century: the emergence of large organizations'. Theories of team management are more relevant here (Catmull, 2014; Sawyer, 2003, 2017; see also Morrow, 2018, pp. 47–49). Kotter (2001) is a change specialist, and so he is inherently biased towards large organisations. Music artist management, by contrast, is most often smaller scale and is organic, adaptable and diversified. It often contrasts with the form of management Kotter is describing, a form that emphasises linearity, conformity and standardisation. In my earlier work (Morrow, 2018), I argued that 'the uniqueness of artist management stems from its subordination to artistic creativities and the fact that such symbolic creativities are artistically/aesthetically autonomous and cannot be reduced to set rules or procedures' (p. 2). In that earlier work, I also argued that artist management was a form of group creativity. Like the yin-yang symbol metaphor mentioned in Chapter 1, which involves visualising the manager as the opposite side of this symbol from the artist, my own attempt to conceptualise artist management was as follows:

> Pluralising creativity enables us to understand that artistic creativity and managerial creativity are different types of creativity that interact with one another in sometimes combustible and conflicting ways, and at other times in generative ones. This also enables artistic creativity to remain unique. . . . Artist management can therefore be defined as a form of group creativity that involves the interaction between artistic creativities and

managerial creativities. Defining artist management in this way enables us to pluralise this form of creativity and to conceptualise it as a dialectic between these two clusters of creativities.

(Morrow, 2018, p. 8)

In the current book I build on this definition by delineating leadership in this context. This is partly to contribute to theory, and partly for pragmatic reasons: what a role is called is important, and—given that leadership can be defined differently to management—there appears to be a disconnection between the fact that many music artist managers define the role as being an artist's CEO—a 'leader'—whereas the role itself is often described as a 'management' one. The work of Alvesson and Sveningsson (2003) is relevant here because it raises the question of whether this mismatch exists because music artist management is more special and extraordinary than it is, or whether leadership itself is often more mundane than it is perceived to be. Alvesson and Sveningsson are critical of the leadership-management distinction, and they noted that the word 'leadership' is sometimes applied to mundane work in attempts to make it seem more remarkable and significant than it is: 'We argue that what managers ('leaders') do may not be that special, but because they are managers doing 'leadership', fairly mundane acts may be given an extraordinary meaning, at least by the managers themselves' (pp. 1437–1438).

The issue in my study was that managers clearly think they are leading when others, such as artists, see them as managing. When it comes to remuneration and the sustainability of the artist-manager relationship, this is a larger issue than it may initially seem.

Music artist leadership

As stated earlier, delineating music artist leadership in this context is not a simple task given the many different types and definitions of leadership. Rather than continuing to conflate management and leadership, better understanding the role leadership specifically plays in the development of an artist's career trajectory is important. Doing so may help to better align the role of a music artist manager with the realities of the contemporary music business: record labels do not lead in the way that they used to; instead they often react to artist-to-fan connections that are facilitated by social media.[3] While record labels may subsequently come on board to help grow such direct connections, it is often the artists themselves and their managers, if they have them, who lead the initial generative process of connecting directly with fans, and they may continue to do so throughout an artist's career.

Even when a record label comes on board, the direct connections between artists and fans are still typically led by the artist and their management. Such social media engagement requires more leadership from managers on a day-to-day basis and was described in the following interview as now involving them being 'always on'. Australian artist manager John Watson explained:

> Artists' careers, and thus managers' careers, used to move more like farming. They moved through cycles. There was a period where you sowed the field, a period where you grew the field, a period where you harvested the field, and a period where you let the field lie fallow, right? You made an album, you released the album, you toured the album, you'd then go away and write the album. So, there was a time when the field lay fallow where everyone could catch their breath, recharge their batteries, regain some perspective, and saddle up again. In a social media world, streaming world, everybody is always on. We're back to the first four years of the The Beatles mentality where every 12 weeks you need a single and ideally another track in between it from now until the end of your career. So, if you're managing an artist, there's that pressure as well and the pressure to be on social media daily. And if you've got an artist who's very active on social media, then that's probably a good news story, though not always . . . you can be good active or you can be bad active.
>
> (Interview 13)

Music artists' careers, as described here, no longer work in album cycles. In the past, these cycles were managed and led by record labels in many instances. According to the following participant, a leading Australian music artist manager, the more frequent release of music and associated audio-visual content now required demands a type of management and leadership that is more nuanced than it was in the past:

> I think social media, generally speaking, has changed everything about the fabric of society, and has, obviously, had a huge impact on every aspect of the music industry . . . the most obvious way in which that has impacted managers is the necessity to produce a lot of audio-visual content . . . it's all very nuanced, very much dependent upon the artist and the manager and the nature of the creative output of each other. But at the end of the day, that pressure exists, for the vast majority of artists, and therefore it translates into a significant amount of added pressure [being placed on] the manager, because of the need for the manager to manage all of that, to really take the lead on helping bring the artist's creative visions to life.
>
> (Interview 2)

In this description of music artist management, the type of leadership that is now required of managers is relatively new. Higgs and Rowland's (2005) work is useful here. They linked literature on leadership behaviour to change management and found that more facilitating and enabling leadership styles are associated with success, rather than leader-centric, directive behaviours.

This participant's comments indicate that helping bring the artist's creative visions to life involves a facilitating and enabling leadership style. Given that music artist managers are taking the lead in helping to bring the artist's creative visions to life through social media, what other aspects of leadership does this involve?

To answer this question, I turned to the work of Lee et al. (2020) who used meta-analysis to compare the relative effects of 13 leadership variables on creativity and innovation. Meta-analysis involves using a quantitative study design to systematically assess previous research studies and derive conclusions about a large body of research. Their work provides an overview of the field of leadership research. It is useful here because this book concerns the interaction between artistic creativity and managerial creativity as well as innovation and how leadership can be delineated within this interaction.

Further, Lee et al. define innovation and creativity as distinct but related constructs. This is useful for an understanding of the role of the music artist manager in the modern music business because, while creativity is 'largely an intrapersonal activity concerned with the generation of truly novel ideas' (Lee et al., 2020, p. 2), 'innovation is a largely interpersonal activity concerned with introducing new ideas (which can come from anyone/anywhere) that fit the context, garnering support from others, and ultimately implementing the new ideas' (p. 2). Music artist management certainly involves innovation in this sense and therefore involves leadership styles that stimulate innovation as well as creativity. The 13 different leadership variables or styles that Lee et al. compared were transformational leadership, transactional leadership, authentic leadership, servant leadership, ethical leadership, humble leadership, empowering leadership, entrepreneurial leadership, LMX (leader-member exchange theory, which is a relationship-based approach to leadership), supportive leadership, benevolent leadership, authoritarian leadership and destructive leadership.

Music artist manager leadership

My examination of leadership styles—and the extent to which they may have positive or negative impacts on the creativity and innovation that is generated within and through the artist-manager relationship—started with a consideration of the artist as a leader. I will now examine the leadership that music artist managers bring to the relationship. This is because, in many ways, the manager is a follower of the artist. Not only does the manager seek remuneration from the artist, but the manager essentially follows the direction set by the artist's talent and ability to engage their audience.

Therefore manager-to-artist leadership involves servant leadership. The concept of servant leadership, and its associated philosophy, was developed by Greenleaf (1970, 1977) and involves putting the needs of followers and stakeholders first: 'The servant-leader is servant first. It begins with the natural feeling that one wants to serve. Then conscious choice brings one to aspire to lead' (Greenleaf, 1970, p. 13).

In theory, the manager does put the needs of the artist and other stakeholders first. The word servant here evokes followership. Obviously, followership is the essential flip side of any leadership, without which the latter cannot properly function. The 'followership' and 'leadership' that exists in the artist-manager relationship alternates depending on the task at hand. The artist and the manager both play the follower role which is the yin to the yang of each other's leadership, and the word servant here simply means serving the long-term interests and vision of the artist.

The concept of servant leadership may initially appear to border on the oxymoronic. Given that in Kotter's (2001) thinking, discussed earlier, leadership concerns developing a vision and strategies to achieve it, servant leadership implies that this is something that 'servants' do. However, the word 'servant' here simply means that such a leader focuses on the needs of others before their own. It is a long-term approach to leadership that aligns with transformational leadership. As I will discuss later, it involves managers transcending self-interest for the greater good of *the artist's* organisation (Lee et al., 2020, p. 2). Therefore, while the manager could be seen as subservient through use of the word 'servant' here, this word simply means that they are engaged in a transformational relationship; they are a servant to the artist's vision, to the ideas they have for the future.

While there is a risk here of overenthusiasm for applying concepts of 'leadership' onto what managers do, thus overlooking less sexy terms such as 'facilitator' or 'coordinator', given that the research participants often self-described their role as the artist's CEO, and given the changing dynamics of the music business mean that managers are carrying more responsibilities than in the past, it is an apt term to describe their role. As outlined earlier, managers are carrying more weight and responsibility than they did in the past, leading the managers that took part in my research to argue that typical management agreements are no longer fit for their purpose. This mismatch between the roles of contemporary managers and the typical management agreements now exists because their role involves more leadership than it did in the past. There has been a shift in power to artists within the music industries and, related to this, a shift in power to those who manage them. For an earlier research project concerning the establishment of a code of conduct for music artist managers through the International Music Managers Forum, in Toronto in 2010, I interviewed an influential Canadian music executive and music artist manager, who noted:

> It's obviously true that there is a bigger focus going to be placed on managers. But on the other hand, it's very difficult for me to say that there could have been any bigger focus than the one that, you know, Colonel Tom Parker had, or Albert Grossman had, or Peter Grant had, or any of the

famous managers in the past had on them. So I guess in general it's true that managers may well be picking up some of the slack that was left with the major record company. But then nobody ever really ended up working with a major record company who didn't have a manager anyway; there's very few examples. So there's always managers there anyway. So I think the real shift of power is to the artists. There should be an artist code of conduct, I think. I think managers are minor players in the scenario you're unfolding, to be truthful. I mean the real fact is it's going to be artists that are going to be the power. So they should have a code of conduct. Good luck.

(Morrow, 2018, p. 76)

It is interesting to note that the one trade body that could arguably establish a music artist code of conduct for their members, the Featured Artists' Coalition (FAC), does not mention a code of conduct on its website. The FAC is a UK trade body that represents 'the specific rights and interests of music artists' (FAC, 2020). In contrast, the AAM has a code of conduct (AAM, n.d.) to which members must adhere.

Unlike the UK which has the FAC, in Australia, according to one music artist manager,

there's no broad integrated artist collective, where they share information and understandings of what's acceptable and what's not, in terms of everything from terms and negotiations of contracts, but right through to behaviour and respect for others. That piece is not shared in a broader collective. So, you are, for into all intents and purposes, dealing with small and isolated groups of people that don't really talk, or know what is acceptable, and what is not.

(Interview 6)

As evidenced by this quotation and the one in Chapter 1 concerning artist-to-manager bullying, this manager clearly does not think that popular music artists are sharing this information through the Media, Entertainment and Arts Alliance (MEAA), which is the largest and most established union and industry advocate for Australia's creative professionals. If the FAC could establish an affiliated organisation in Australia that could exist alongside MEAA, this could help to mitigate this issue. Further, there is literature from the field of arts and cultural management concerning shared leadership through the artistic director-general manager relationship in arts organisations that could be useful here (see, for example, Inglis & Cray, 2011).

Thus, rather than solely focusing on motivating forms of leadership here, it is necessary to better understand ineffective or negative leadership. Lee et al. (2020) focused on two leadership styles—authoritarian and destructive—to expand our understanding of the impact negative leadership has on creativity and innovation. While all leadership styles can potentially be negative and authoritarian, leadership is only negative if the followers do not agree with the outcomes. My argument here is that authoritarian leadership is not a model that suits creative work. An authoritarian leader 'asserts absolute authority and control over subordinates and demands unquestionable obedience' (Cheng et al., 2004, p. 91, as cited in Lee et al., 2020, p. 4). This controlling type of leader dictates structures and rules while promising rewards for compliance and threatening punishment for non-compliance (Aryee et al., 2007). Pellegrini and Scandura (2008) found that followers of such leaders are less likely to use their own initiative to generate novel approaches to their work. Operating under such conditions of absolute control and the fear and caution that accompany them impairs employee creativity and innovation.

Destructive leadership occurs when leaders intentionally commit harmful acts towards followers including rudeness, breaking promises, mocking and belittlement (Tepper, 2000). This type of leadership involves an abusive style of supervision that provokes fear (Kiewitz et al., 2016). Psychological resources that might otherwise be channelled into the creation of novel and useful ideas are instead consumed by attempts to manage the stress caused by such abusive supervision. Followers subject to this abuse often experience emotional exhaustion (Wu & Hu, 2009). Both authoritarian and destructive leadership styles negatively impact the motivation and autonomy of music artist managers and can exacerbate their burnout.

Autonomy—the capacity to make one's own decisions and determine the course of one's own life—is an important concept here and is arguably a key reason why some music artist managers feel subject to destructive leadership from artists. Such feelings relate to 'respect', which involves recognising and acknowledging that individuals have value in themselves, and that this value should inform interactions between artists and managers. Such respect includes recognising the value of human autonomy. In the case of artist-to-manager leadership, though, this respect for autonomy is fiendishly difficult for the artist to recognise and grant because the manager is managing the artist—a person who is also the product, or a group of people that are also the product. The result is that managers are arguably more likely to be micromanaged by their client artists than to have their autonomy supported.

This disregard for or negation of a manager's autonomy happens for two key reasons. First, no matter how enamoured a manager may be with the artist's creative work, it is the artist's work and their career. Second, artists often over-identify with their work because they themselves are so enamoured by it and the psychological state of flow (Csikszentmihalyi, 2008) they get into while creating it. Artists may find it difficult to psychologically detach or refrain from thinking about their work. Managers, by contrast, often have multiple clients. So artists tend to think about their own work more than their manager thinks about the same work. Further, there is a certain fragility to artists' careers, and so artists are often over-identifying with something that is fragile. In their influential book concerning creative labour, Hesmondhalgh and Baker (2011) argued that this type of labour often involves '"self-exploitation", whereby workers become so enamoured with their jobs that they push themselves to the limits of their physical and emotional endurance' (p. 6). The fact that the manager is managing the 'concrete and named labour of the artist' (Ryan, 1992, p. 41) means that the product they are managing is a person, or group of people, and this person or group may be prone to the obsessive overwork that stems from over-identification with work, and this can lead to the artist self-exploiting.

An artist's self-exploitation can then have flow-on effects for managers in several ways. Not only can managers get caught up in such a whirlwind of overwork, but such self-exploiting artists are also likely to want to micromanage every aspect of their career. Amabile (1998), a leading creativity and leadership researcher, argued against micromanagement, observing that 'people will be more creative . . . if you give them freedom to decide how to climb a particular mountain' (p. 81). This means that leaders should set goals but not micromanage the process of achieving the goals. However, in the case of music artist management, artists may be too anxious and hesitant to grant their manager autonomy in their work because the mountain they are trying to climb is *their* (the artist's) career.

This is the 'autonomy hurdle' of music artist management. The value of human autonomy—to reiterate, the capacity to make one's own decisions and determine the course of one's own life—can more easily be understood when thinking about artists in the artist-manager relationship than managers. If respect for managers as people involves allowing them due scope, throughout the leadership process, to make their own decisions, then this is difficult to manage because the ultimate decision-making rests with the artist. Boundary setting in the artist-manager relationship therefore requires developing an understanding of the scope within which managers can make *their* own decisions. Differentiation of the decisions required for setting the goals for the artist's career, and those required throughout the process of achieving those goals, could help with this boundary setting.

In contrast to negative leadership, motivating leadership that is both empowering and entrepreneurial involves the leader communicating their confidence in their followers' work, and acknowledging its significance by encouraging self-directed and autonomous decision-making through the delegation of authority (Kirkman & Rosen, 1999). Such self-determination can trigger intrinsic motivation—'the incentive we feel to complete a task simply because we find it interesting or enjoyable' (Falk, 2023)—which can in turn lead to autonomous exploration and unique solutions to problems (Li & Zhang, 2016). These solutions concern different approaches to music artist management. Autonomy, which is otherwise known as self-determination, is therefore important for music artist management to be good, motivating and enjoyable work; autonomy therefore can be defined as a psychological need that managers have.

Good, enjoyable and fulfilling work in music artist management

So, can music artist management be good, enjoyable and fulfilling work for music artist managers? When asked what is good about their work, what motivates them and why they continue in the role, the managers I interviewed responded:

> Our industry is the greatest thing to be in. It's so much fun, we all love the music, we love being involved with creative, free minded people, we're not stuck in large corporations, dictating our life in a way, which could make us mundane and lose our spark. That's why we're here, the love of music and also [the] lifestyle.
>
> (Interview 1)

> It's an incredible profession, and one that utilises every skill you could possibly have, from business to event planning, to marketing, to promotion to sales. It's all there. It's the best grounding you could possibly have as a generalist in the world of work and, on top of that, you get the benefit of having that intimate involvement with an artist.
>
> (Interview 6)

> The most wonderful and life affirming part of it is being at a live show. And seeing that audience connection with an artist on stage and seeing all of that work that you do behind the scenes every day, tangibly, in front of you.
>
> (Interview 6)

> I think the reward is being able to work in an industry that you love . . . music can do so much and create change. It is such a powerful thing.
>
> (Interview 7)

> It allows you also to work around other things. I've got three kids, and I'm able to pick them up from school every day and take them to school every day.
>
> (Interview 7)

> It's just incredibly varied . . . it just could not be more varied from day to day and within a day.
>
> (Interview 6)

> You get to meet and work with a lot of different people. You get to travel around this country, and if you're lucky, travel around the world. You get to watch these careers grow from grassroots, playing to 100 people to then

start to play in these large venues to 1,000 people, and you get to be there for the whole ride, which is just amazing.

(Interview 9)

I think the positive experiences are being able to be creative, working with really interesting people by whom one can be inspired. When the artists get to a certain level of income, it can be quite financially rewarding.

(Interview 11)

The opportunity to earn a good living without the structure of an office job is a huge positive.

(Interview 12)

I think if you love the creative process of music, and you believe, fundamentally, in the value of music creation, then managers are in the box seat, as the navigators of the career . . . it also is a role that keeps you on your toes. You're constantly learning. The business is a rapidly changing business. The businesses, really, all the businesses, the live business, the publishing business, social media business, they're all different businesses, and they're all changing, and the manager has to be able to keep up with that change.

(Interview 13)

When the industry is a bit smaller . . . you get to know everybody, and it's inherently fun. It's quite social. We work in entertainment. So, attending shows, making cool things, seeing what other people are doing, bouncing ideas off each other. Inherently we're in the business of entertaining people and so the end product is very enjoyable.

(Interview 14)

What is good about working in artist management is the absolute joy that you get from working closely with an artist as they progressively keep achieving goals and reaching milestones and, essentially, realising their potential as a creator . . . being so close to that creative process is, yeah, it's a really beautiful thing.

(Interview 15)

Well, the positive obviously, is potentially financial, if you have a very successful artist.

(Interview 16)

I think what draws me to artist management is the notion of close relationships. Creative, strategic, creating a framework for the artist to thrive and do what they're really good at, bring their vision to life. And build a team around that to have that moment where you hear that demo, and then it's on radio, see that show where they're supporting that band, and then they've played their own, sold out a 100 capacity venue, to them playing in front of 5000 people or playing mainstage on Splendour [Splendour in the Grass Festival], that moment is just euphoric, and amazing.

(Interview 3)

What is good about management is the closeness. It's about, for me person- ally, I guess it's about association and ownership of what someone else called recently 'psychic income'. So not actual financial income, but the income of being a part of something that's meaningful that actually contributes to soci- ety and means something to other people or connects you to other people.

(Interview 5)

I just call it the fire in my belly, it's like falling in love. You just can't do sensible things when you fall in love. [It's] something that you truly believe in, and that you think more people need to experience in life before you die.

(Interview 5)

To analyse these responses, I will now turn to self-determination theory (SDT) and will link this to the leadership theories introduced earlier. Deci and Ryan (2012) explained that 'self-determination theory (SDT) is an empiri- cally derived theory of human motivation and personality in social contexts that differentiates motivation in terms of being autonomous and controlled' (p. 417). According to SDT, autonomy, relatedness and competence are three universal psychological needs that are essential for optimal personal devel- opment and functioning. Just as when it comes to the facilitation of creativ- ity and innovation, as outlined earlier, negative leadership is associated with control and micromanagement, and motivating leadership involves the leader encouraging self-directed and autonomous decision-making, autonomy takes primacy in SDT with autonomy-supportive leadership also supporting follow- ers' competence and relatedness needs.

Relatedness involves the desire to feel connected to others, loved and meaningfully involved with the broader social world. Alongside relatedness and autonomy in SDT is the psychological need for a sense of competence, the demonstrated ability to do something efficiently and successfully. For Deci and Ryan (2012) these three basic psychological needs—autonomy, related- ness and competence—are interrelated. For example, the authors define autonomy support as 'taking the others' perspective, encouraging initiation and exploration, providing choice, and being responsive' (p. 426). Therefore,

authorities who support autonomy also tend to support competence and relatedness, so it is often the case that, when autonomy is being supported, competence and relatedness are also being supported, although satisfaction of each need is associated with independent influences and resulting dynamic outcomes.

(p. 427)

In the responses earlier to the questions of what is good about their work, what motivates them and why they continue in the role, the participants' comments can be mapped onto these psychological needs in the following ways.

The participants' responses here align with SDT. Music artist management can be good work by fulfilling the three universal psychological needs that are essential for optimal development and functioning: autonomy, relatedness

Table 2.1 Mapping participants' comments to psychological needs

Psychological need	Participants'comments
Autonomy	'Fun, creative, free-minded.'
	'Not stuck in large corporations, dictating our life.'
	'The love of music and also [the] lifestyle.'
	'It allows you also to work around other things.'
	'The opportunity to earn a good living without the structure of an office job is a huge positive.'
Relatedness	'Intimate involvement with an artist.'
	'Seeing that audience connection with an artist on stage.'
	'Music can do so much and create change.'
	'You get to meet and work with a lot of different people.'
	'I think the positive experiences are being able to be creative, working with really interesting people by whom one can be inspired.'
	'When the industry is a bit smaller . . . you get to know everybody, and it's inherently fun. It's quite social.'
	'What is good about working in artist management is the absolute joy that you get from working closely with an artist.'
	'Being so close to that creative process is, yeah, it's a really beautiful thing.'
	'Close relationships.'
	'What is good about management is the closeness.'
	'Being a part of something that's meaningful that actually contributes to society and means something to other people or connects you to other people.'
	'[It's] something that you truly believe in, and that you think more people need to experience in life before you die.'
Competence	'It's an incredible profession, and one that utilises every skill you could possibly have.'
	'It's just incredibly varied . . . it just could not be more varied from day to day and within a day.'
	'It also is a role that keeps you on your toes. You're constantly learning. The business is a rapidly changing business.'

and competence. Interestingly, out of these three needs, more comments have been included in the box earlier for 'relatedness' than the other two boxes. The participants articulated a special type of relatedness that involves artistic creativity. The psychological need for relatedness is managers' key motivation. This need is met when the role provides managers with a sense of belonging to a broader community, a strong connection to artists and being so close to the artistically creative[4] process that managers feel meaningfully involved with their social environments. This relatedness occurs particularly through the way in which artists in turn connect with their audiences, and the way that music managers help to create and lead change within these social structures.

The participants' comments also map onto autonomy because music artist management is often relatively small scale and is organic, adaptable and diversified, contrasting with other forms of management that emphasise linearity, conformity and standardisation. The need for a sense of competence is also met when managers are called on to bring multiple skills to the competent completion of their work across a diverse portfolio of activities. Their capacity is also stretched through having to deal with constant change, and this can provide them with a very broad and evolving feeling of competence. Australian music artist manager Keith Welsh discussed both autonomy and competence in the following quotation:

> I think there's a certain flexibility about doing this kind of job rather than doing something that's, say, more office bound. I like working for myself with my clients. So, I never see myself working for anybody. I see myself as working with people. I also think, because there are creative challenges coming up all the time, and because there are different projects all the time, it's not a single idea. So, there are multiple skills that are needed and multiple problems to solve week by week.
>
> (Interview 11)

The sense of autonomy pervading the interviews often related to the structure of the managers' working time, though this can have a downside too as managers are prone to self-exploitation. Welsh continued: 'I think that some of the other negatives are the hours. I've got a really horrible boss, me, so, I don't take holidays, and I'm always on call' (Interview 11).

While this manager had a sense of autonomy because they perceived that they are their own boss, there was still a sense that the artists they work *with*, rather than *for*, operate in artistically/aesthetically autonomous ways, and the manager is subordinate to this type of autonomy: 'The negatives are . . . Having to rely on the whims of clients—and I know that's not just the music business—but having to rely on the whims of clients who are creators who may change their mind' (Interview 11).

There clearly are contextual factors that enable some participants' needs to be met. At best, managers do work in autonomy-supportive contexts in which they are provided with choice, where their personal initiative is encouraged and their competence is supported in a climate of relatedness (Deci et al., 2001; Gagné, 2003). This is why most participant comments listed earlier concern autonomous motivation (e.g., intrinsic motivation) as opposed to controlled motivation (e.g., extrinsic motivation, for example, financial reward). While some comments did relate to extrinsic motivation—'It's a model where you don't invest financially, and the ceiling is quite high and that's unique in the business world'; 'When the artists get to a certain level of income, it can be quite financially rewarding'; 'Well, the positive obviously, is potentially financial, if you have a very successful artist'—it is clear from this research that, for the managers who participated, the primary motivation is intrinsic. While managers are entrepreneurial, 'You get to watch these careers grow', key words that stood out in the responses to the questions concerning what is good about their work, what motivates them and why they continue in the role were 'music', 'love', 'creative', 'euphoric' and 'amazing'. Australian-Canadian music artist manager Michael McMartin summed up what is good about working in music artist management in the following way:

> The intangible enjoyment of the feedback you get from the work that you do, hearing it and seeing it. I don't know many people that have got into it for the money. They do it for the love of the music and the association with the artists. And having that feedback is by far the most enjoyable aspect. The blessing that comes with income being derived from that, if you're lucky enough, is certainly the icing on the cake.
>
> (Interview 12)

A needs-supportive framework for artist-to-manager leadership therefore needs to involve a consideration of both financial rewards and non-financial rewards. If the psychological need for relatedness is a key motivation, and if this partly involves a strong connection to the artist, artists providing positive feedback and choice through their leadership of managers could help to further fulfil this need.

While there is clearly a need to critically examine music artist management agreements and therefore address the issue of financial reward management, a focus on non-financial rewards is also needed to deal with cultural issues in the field. One high-profile Australian music artist who participated in the aforementioned panel that AAM produced and that I chaired for BIG-SOUND festival and conference in 2022, Oscar Dawson, who was introduced earlier, engaged in the following conversation with Australian artist manager and current AAM Co-Chair Jess Keeley. Following on from a discussion of a perceived mass exodus of talented music artist managers from the music business, these two participants engaged in the following dialogue:

> Oscar Dawson: The exodus that we're talking about, do you think that that would be reversed purely by money? Or is it also a cultural thing as well?

Jess Keeley: Massively cultural. Yeah, it has to be cultural before it's financial.

Oscar Dawson: In some of the discussions we talked about the financial incentives, etc., and that's important, but it's not just that is it? Is it also the way the managers are treated?

Jess Keeley: Yes, the workload. We're at the beginning of some of these conversations. And I do feel like it's this cultural transparency moment. So, because when I think about going in and having a conversation with a record label right now, on behalf of an artist, I think that, again, we're like, invisible, this management role is invisible.

(Dawson et al., 2022)

In line with these panel participants' comments, a needs-supportive framework for artist-to-manager leadership first needs to consider non-financial rewards and lift the lid on cultural issues that exist in the treatment of managers, through a 'cultural transparency moment'. Once managers' needs have been made more visible, financial reward could be considered within a healthier environment. This approach is potentially powerful. Deci and Ryan (2012) found that 'positive feedback and choice were predicted to enhance experiences of competence and self-determination, fostering greater intrinsic motivation, and results have confirmed this as well' (p. 419), whereas 'monetary rewards, threats, and competition were predicted to thwart autonomy, and such events did typically undermine intrinsic motivation' (p. 419). In this context though, financial reward management and non-financial reward management are interrelated; a financial reward structure that makes managers relatively disposable influences how they are treated and how they feel about their roles.

Non-financial rewards are also fundamental because, as the participants explained, financial rewards are often off on a distant horizon somewhere; and because they are often so far off, better, more immediate financial reward structures are needed to address the distrust and fear that can creep into artist-manager relationships. Distrust arises because the artist may be poached by another manager before the financial reward on the horizon is realised. Artist-to-manager leadership of the type encapsulated in the management agreements outlined in Chapter 1 can be thought of as involving transformational leadership[5] because artists as leaders influence managers as followers to transcend self-interest for the greater good of *their* organisation (Lee et al., 2020, p. 2). In these agreements, at first there is little or no financial reward for artist managers because the compensation is deferred and paid in commissions.

Managers agree to these terms for a few reasons. First, artists often do not have much money when they are starting out; second, competition with other managers to sign artists means there is a race to the bottom on management fees; and third, the psychological need for relatedness is the key motivation. At such times, managers are often seeking a connection with the artist, a sense of belonging to a valued community and a feeling of being meaningfully involved in desirable social circles. This meaningful connection with artists through which both parties may feel that they are in it together can, according to one participant, have a downside later on regarding financial rewards. Even when the manager is established, there is an expectation that they will transcend self-interest for the greater good by waiving management commissions on loss-making tours:

> With touring, I think that's the area where the commission structure gets really difficult, because that actually can be quite profitable for a manager. I've had a bunch of tours where turnover's been 800 grand [AUD 800,000], you know, 500 grand [AUD 500,000], and if you're taking it straight off the top, you can be making pretty significant money. And, depending on your staff costs, it's like, 'Okay, this is making sense'. The obvious problem being [that] the artist might, on that same tour, have lost 100 grand [AUD 100,000] and it's just so difficult to kind of go, like, 'All right. Nah, I'm still gonna charge full rate, or any rate', you know.[6] It's common for people to be like, 'You can't commission a loss-making tour'. But obviously you're working, you don't have any ownership in the business and, you know, big managers are like, 'Nah, we'd never commission a loss-making tour'. But most international tours are loss making. And they're hard, hard fucking work . . . and often you're turning up there, you're buying your own flights, all that stuff. So, you can end up making a good loss on this tour as a manager.
>
> (Interview 8)

While a manager's transcending of self-interest may partly stem from their psychological need for relatedness and the unique working relationship they have with their client, competition between managers may be a factor as well.

Established managers or management firms saying that they would 'never commission a loss-making tour' contributes to a race to the bottom on financial rewards for managers more generally. At its worst, such discourse can feed into an attempt by one manager to poach a client from another. In the scenario outlined earlier, this can, in turn, feed into a manager's anxiety about whether they should even have the audacity to invoice for the commission that they are owed according to the management agreement they have with their client. According to the following participant, this issue can be exacerbated by cultural differences between territories as well. While this participant described the membership of the AAM as being a 'beautiful management community' (Interview 1), they went on to state that the relatively insecure nature of artist management agreements like the one outlined in Chapter 1 can lead to a situation whereby

> if you've spent any time in America, this leads to the most horrible behaviour from human beings that I've ever seen. Because I've seen, you know, the poachers, the manager poachers who undermine the current manager

and say untruthful things. The tactics are horrific, because it's a cowboy industry where you can steal things from people, if in the end, the artist is vulnerable to hearing things. And we don't have that here. We've got a very honourable community, I believe. But you look at where it goes. I've gone to America, and I've experienced this myself and heard from so many of my colleagues. It's terrible.

(Interview 1)

While, as outlined earlier, the social environment in which managers operate can be a good, needs-supportive one, the social environment they operate in can also be a toxic one in which relatedness and connection are replaced with a complete lack of trust.

Manager-to-artist leadership is one way in which this absence of trust can be addressed. One dimension of transformational leadership is inspirational motivation; this involves articulating an appealing and inspiring vision (Lee et al., 2020). Just as by working with a board, a CEO has a role in articulating such a vision, manager-to-artist leadership involves this process of envisioning as well. One example of this in action was provided by the participant introduced earlier who discussed the waiving of management commissions on loss-making tours. While for this manager, articulating a vision was key, this needs to be followed with the transparency and communication required to lead the artist through this difficult scenario. For this participant, this involves the manager saying:

'Sometimes I've got to have the guts to show an artist a budget that's losing 20 grand [AUD 20,000], and to tell them, 'I still think this tour really makes sense doing, but I'll make 20 grand [AUD 20,000] if I take full commission and you're gonna lose 20 grand [AUD 20,000]. Are you going to sign off on that?' To have a relationship where someone can have an artist who has perspective to say, 'All right, this might feel shit, but I can see the big picture that I own this business and I think this is going to move my business forward. It's going to increase the value of my intellectual property and in the long run I'm going to increase fees and profile and it's going to head in this direction. You're working on it now as a contractor on a commission basis. Of course, you need to be paid.'

(Interview 8)

In this example, the psychological contract—the implicit, unwritten and intangible elements of the artist-manager relationship—is quite different to the written management agreement. How both parties understand their relationship outside of the written agreement outlined in Chapter 1 dramatically impacts the music artist manager's remuneration, despite what is agreed in writing. This participant continued on the subject of managers commissioning loss-making tours due to having adjusted gross rather than net live commission clauses in their written agreements:

> I'd say it's rare that an artist understands that and that a manager can stay firm on that. We often blame ourselves and feel like we're not doing a good job because the tour is losing money . . . it's incredibly tough . . . [and it is] very hard to charge for your work in this scenario. Some people are comfortable with it, but my experience is that many more are not, and this presents a problem for the commission model on live touring especially.
>
> (Interview 8)

It can obviously be difficult for managers who are running the artist's business to pay everyone else who worked on a tour but not themselves (usually via a separate business manager on large tours) because of an unwritten understanding with the artist and a culture in the field whereby managers generally do not commission loss-making tours. While the upside is that it makes the artist's business easier for them to run if there is one less expense, in this instance a premium is placed on non-financial rewards for managers to stay motivated and continue in their role.

Conclusion

In this chapter I engaged with literature from the fields of reward management, leadership and social psychology to address the core research problem that is driving this book: to what extent is it possible for managers to do good, enjoyable and fulfilling work in music artist management? It is possible for managers to do such work. The participants' responses indicated that music artist management work can meet the three psychological needs that are essential for optimal development and functioning: autonomy, relatedness and competence. There are, however, numerous factors that limit the extent to which doing good, enjoyable and fulfilling work is possible in the role.

These problems include a serious lack of knowledge of human resources theory in the field, leadership reluctance on the part of artists through to a complete lack of awareness that they have a leadership role, the social comparison process through which managers feel a sense of injustice when considering record producer agreements, a lack of trust in the artist and other managers who may poach them, being subject to authoritarian and destructive leadership styles, the 'autonomy hurdle' of music artist management and the fact that the psychological contract can be quite different to the written management agreement, and this can lead to managers not being fully and fairly paid for their work. In the next chapter I build on the notion of artist-to-manager leadership presented in this chapter, which involves a transformational leadership style, to further address these issues and challenges relating to management work in the music business and the servant leadership this work involves.

Notes

1 Oscar Dawson is a composer, songwriter, musician and producer, based in Melbourne, Australia, who currently plays in the band Holy Holy.
2 Synchronisation (sync) licensing involves song publishers or 'sync agents' working to generate fees by having the songs in their catalogue synchronised with moving visual imagery in films, TV shows and advertisements.
3 See Hughes et al. (2016, pp. 28–32) for an outline of the shift from linear to circular career development for artists in the music industries that has occurred due to the digitisation of these industries and the emergence of social media.
4 I use the term 'artistically creative' here because there are different types of creativity, and I am emphasising that this is just one type. For example, as discussed in this book, managerial creativity is a different type of creativity.
5 Lee et al. (2020) noted that: 'Transformational leadership (Bass, 1985) consists of four dimensions: idealized influence (i.e., leader behaviour that is admirable and charismatic), inspirational motivation (i.e., articulating an appealing and inspiring vision), intellectual stimulation (i.e., challenging follower assumptions and listening to their ideas), and individualized consideration (i.e., mentoring and coaching according to followers' unique needs)' (p. 2).
6 The reason why the manager and artist are in different financial positions here relates to the clause in the management agreement concerning live performance income and the question of what is deducted from gross income before the manager's commission. See the outline in Chapter 1. This participant also said: 'I think you've got an issue with the fact that the UK managers are commissioning on net, and the US managers are commissioning on gross but often at a lower percentage. Globally, everyone has got slightly different models, and it makes things uncomfortable when the landscape is global and artists are often working globally' (Interview 8).

References

Allen, P. (2018). *Artist management for the music business* (4th ed.). Routledge.
Alvesson, M., & Sveningsson, S. (2003). Managers doing leadership: The extra-ordinarization of the mundane. *Human Relations, 56*(12), 1435–1459. https://doi.org/10.1177/00187267035612001
Amabile, T. M. (1998, September 1). How to kill creativity. *Harvard Business Review*. https://hbr.org/1998/09/how-to-kill-creativity
Anderton, C., Dubber, A., & James, M. (2013). *Understanding the music industries*. SAGE. https://doi.org/10.4135/9781473915008
Antoni, C. H. (2019). Psychological perspectives on reward management. In S. J. Perkins (Ed.), *The Routledge companion to reward management* (pp. 16–24). Routledge.

Armstrong, M., & Murlis, H. (2007). *Reward Management: A Handbook of Remuneration Strategy and Practice*. Kogan Page Publishers.

Aryee, S., Chen, Z. X., Sun, L.-Y., & Debrah, Y. A. (2007). Antecedents and outcomes of abusive supervision: Test of a trickle-down model. *Journal of Applied Psychology*, *92*(1), 191–201. https://doi.org/10.1037/0021-9010.92.1.191

Association of Artist Managers (AAM). (n.d.). *About*. www.aam.org.au/about

Bass, B. M., & Riggio, R. E. (2005). *Transformational leadership: A comprehensive review of theory and research* (2nd ed.). Psychology Press.

Bennis, W. G. (2009). *On becoming a leader*. Hachette UK.

Bilton, C., & Leary, R. (2002). What can managers do for creativity? Brokering creativity in the creative industries. *International Journal of Cultural Policy*, *8*(1), 49–64. https://doi.org/10.1080/10286630290032431

Brown, D. (2019). New realism in 'strategic' reward management: Bringing together research and practice. In S. J. Perkins (Ed.), *The Routledge companion to reward management* (pp. 55–71). Routledge.

Catmull, E. (2014). *Creativity, Inc: Overcoming the unseen forces that stand in the way of true inspiration*. Random House.

Chaparro, G., & Musgrave, G. (2021). Moral music management: Ethical decision-making after Avicii. *International Journal of Music Business Research*, *10*(1), 3–16. https://doi.org/10.2478/ijmbr-2021-0001

Csikszentmihalyi, M. (2008). *Flow: The psychology of optimal experience*. Harper Perennial.

Dannen, F. (1991). *Hit men: Power brokers and fast money inside the music business*. Knopf Doubleday Publishing Group.

Dawson, O., Keeley, J., & Carey, G. (2022, September 7). *Sustainable relationships? The value of management partnerships* [Panel presentation, G. Morrow, Chair]. BigSound, Brisbane, Queensland.

Deci, E. L., & Ryan, R. M. (2012). Self-determination theory. In P. A. M. Van Lange, A. W. Kruglanski., & E. T. Higgins (Eds.), *Handbook of theories of social psychology: Volume 1* (pp. 416–436). SAGE. https://doi.org/10.4135/9781446249215

Deci, E. L., Ryan, R. M., Gagné, M., Leone, D. R., Usunov, J., & Kornazheva, B. P. (2001). Need satisfaction, motivation, and well-being in the work organizations of a former Eastern bloc country: A cross-cultural study of self-determination. *Personality and Social Psychology Bulletin*, *27*(8), 930–942. https://doi.org/10.1177/0146167201278002

Druker, J., & White, G. (2009). Introduction. In G. White & J. Druker (Eds.), *Reward management: A critical text* (2nd ed., pp. 1–22). Routledge.

Falk, S. (2023, March 8). Understanding the power of intrinsic motivation. *Harvard Business Review*. https://hbr.org/2023/03/understand-the-power-of-intrinsic-motivation

Featured Artists Coalition. (2020). *Featured artists coalition*. https://thefac.org

Frascogna, X. M., & Hetherington, H. L. (2011). *This business of artist management: The standard reference to all phases of managing a musician's career from both the artist's and manager's point of view*. Crown.

Gagné, M. (2003). The role of autonomy support and autonomy orientation in prosocial behavior engagement. *Motivation and Emotion*, *27*(3), 199–223. https://doi.org/10.1023/A:1025007614869

Gilenson, H. I. (1990). Badlands: Artist—personal manager conflicts of interest in the music industry. *Cardozo Arts & Entertainment Law Journal, 9,* 501–544.

Goodwin, K. (2020). Leadership reluctance in the Australian arts and cultural sector. *Journal of Arts Management, Law, and Society, 50*(3), 169–183. https://doi/org/10.1080/10632921.2020.1739184

Greenleaf, R. K. (1970). *The servant as leader.* Greenleaf Center for Servant Leadership.

Greenleaf, R. K. (1977). *Servant leadership: A journey into the nature of legitimate power and greatness.* Paulist Press.

Hertz, B. W. (1988). The regulation of artist representation in the entertainment industry. *Loyola Entertainment Law Journal, 8,* 55–73.

Hesmondhalgh, D., & Baker, S. (2011). *Creative labour: Media work in three cultural industries.* Routledge.

Higgs, M., & Rowland, D. (2005). All changes great and small: Exploring approaches to change and its leadership. *Journal of Change Management, 5*(2), 121–151. https://doi.org/10.1080/14697010500082902

Hughes, D., Evans, M., Morrow, G., & Keith, S. (2016). *The new music industries.* Springer International Publishing. https://doi.org/10.1007/978-3-319-40364-9

Inglis, L., & Cray, D. (2011). Leadership in Australian arts organisations: A shared experience? *Third Sector Review, 17*(2), 107–130.

Jones, M. L. (2012). *The music industries.* Palgrave Macmillan UK. https://doi.org/10.1057/9781137027061

Kiewitz, C., Restubog, S. L. D., Shoss, M. K., Garcia, P. R. J. M., & Tang, R. L. (2016). Suffering in silence: Investigating the role of fear in the relationship between abusive supervision and defensive silence. *Journal of Applied Psychology, 101*(5), 731–742. https://doi.org/10.1037/apl0000074

Kirkman, B. L., & Rosen, B. (1999). Beyond self-management: Antecedents and consequences of team empowerment. *Academy of Management Journal, 42*(1), 58–74. https://doi.org/10.2307/256874

Kotter, J. P. (2000). What leaders really do. *The Bottom Line, 13*(1). https://doi.org/10.1108/bl.2000.17013aae.001

Kotter, J. P. (2001, December 1). What leaders really do. *Harvard Business Review.* https://hbr.org/2001/12/what-leaders-really-do

Krasilovsky, M. W., & Meloni, R. S. (1990). Ethical considerations for music industry professionals. *Columbia-VLA Journal of Law & the Arts, 15,* 335–365.

Lee, A., Legood, A., Hughes, D., Wei Tian, A., Newman, A., & Knight, C. (2020). Leadership, creativity and innovation: A meta-analytic review. *European Journal of Work and Organizational Psychology, 29*(1), 1–35. https://doi.org/10.1080/1359432X.2019.1661837

Li, M., & Zhang, P. (2016). Stimulating learning by empowering leadership: Can we achieve cross-level creativity simultaneously? *Leadership & Organization Development Journal, 37*(8), 1168–1186. https://doi.org/10.1108/LODJ-01-2015-0007

Morrow, G. (2006). *Managerial creativity: A study of artist management practices in the Australian popular music industry* [Doctoral thesis, Macquarie University]. Figshare. https://figshare.mq.edu.au/articles/thesis/

Managerial_creativity_a_study_of_artist_management_practices_in_the_ Australian_popular_music_industry/19427489

Morrow, G. (2013). Regulating artist managers: An insider's perspective. *International Journal of Music Business Research, 2*(2), 8–35.

Morrow, G. (2018). *Artist management: Agility in the creative and cultural industries.* Routledge.

O'Brien, J. M. (1992). Regulation of attorneys under California's Talent Agencies Act: A tautological approach to protecting artists. *California Law Review, 80*(2), 471–511.

Pellegrini, E. K., & Scandura, T. A. (2008). Paternalistic leadership: A review and agenda for future research. *Journal of Management, 34*(3), 566–593. https://doi.org/10.1177/0149206308316063

Perkins, S. J. (2019). Whither reward management theory research and practice? The essential companion. In S. J. Perkins (Ed.), *The Routledge companion to reward management* (pp. 1–7). Routledge.

Rogan, J. (1988). *Starmakers and Svengalis: The history of British pop management.* Trans-Atlantic.

Ryan, B. (1992). *Making capital from culture: The corporate form of capitalist cultural production.* De Gruyter. https://doi.org/10.1515/9783110847185

Sawyer, K. (2017). *Group genius: The creative power of collaboration.* Hachette UK.

Sawyer, R. K. (2003). *Group creativity: Music, theater, collaboration.* Lawrence Erlbaum Associates.

Tepper, B. J. (2000). Consequences of abusive supervision. *Academy of Management Journal, 43*(2), 178–190. https://doi.org/10.2307/1556375

Weiss, M., & Gaffney, P. (2012). *Managing artists in pop music: What every artist and manager must know to succeed* (3rd ed.). Allworth.

Williamson, J. (2016). Artist managers and entrepreneurship: Risk-takers or risk averse? In A. Dumbreck & G. McPherson (Eds.), *Music entrepreneurship* (pp. 87–112). Bloomsbury Publishing.

Wu, T.-Y., & Hu, C. (2009). Abusive supervision and employee emotional exhaustion: Dispositional antecedents and boundaries. *Group & Organization Management, 34*(2), 143–169. https://doi.org/10.1177/1059601108331217

3 Management work in the music business

Issues and challenges

Summary of the survey of music artist managers

Seventy-seven AAM members completed the survey questionnaire distributed for this book. Most participants in the survey, 87.5 per cent, identified as being serious or professional music artist managers. 'Serious' was based on a self-assessed commitment to music artist management work as a major aspect of the music artist manager's working life, even if this work was not the main source of income. 'Professional' was defined as referring to a level of training, experience or talent and a manner of working that qualified music artist managers to have their work judged against the professional standards of the occupation. Eighty-one per cent of respondents believed that management agreements with artists need to change and evolve. On a positive note, and perhaps unsurprisingly given the end of COVID-19 pandemic-related lockdowns in the live music sector, 43 per cent of participants indicated that there had been an increase in revenue for their management business in 2022. The AAM membership level of the participants was as follows: general 62%, associate 19% (early career managers) and executive 19% (established, successful managers).

Sixty per cent of participants identified as male, 38 per cent female and 2 per cent as gender variant/non-conforming. No participants identified as being of Aboriginal and/or Torres Strait Islander descent. Fourteen per cent indicated that they were from a culturally diverse background. More than three-quarters (79 per cent) of Australian music artist managers who responded reside in a capital city, reflecting the fact that major metropolitan centres are where music business infrastructure tends to be concentrated. Most participants were based in either New South Wales or Victoria, and 69 per cent were 45 years old or younger.

The music artist managers who participated in the survey are more highly educated than the Australian population at large: 62 per cent of respondents hold a university degree, compared to only 32 per cent overall of people aged 15–74 years who hold a bachelor's degree (ABS, 2022). Beyond this general education, as is discussed further in the full survey report (see Morrow &

DOI: 10.4324/9781003388005-4

Long, 2022), the participants spoke of the role the AAM plays, and could play, in having music artist managers' skills recognised with certification; facilitating mentoring and networking opportunities; providing a library of resources and training programs; and sparking innovation in terms of more co-operative ways of working that could help disseminate knowledge from peer to peer.

Other key quantitative data gleaned through the survey included the following: 47 per cent operate as sole traders, while 45 per cent operate through companies; the average number of years working as an artist manager was 10; average annual business revenue was AUD 186,399 (2021–22); the average self-assessed level of management skill was seven out of ten; the average number of artists being managed was five; 75 per cent of music artist managers boost their personal incomes outside the sector; and 75 per cent of the participants receive no public funding for their music artist management work.

This survey was conducted alongside the BIGSOUND 2022 panel that the AAM organised and that was discussed in Chapter 2. As discussed in the prologue to this book, the premise of this panel was the belief that, even before the COVID-19 pandemic, music artist managers were facing a crisis of sustainability that has been exacerbated since 2020. The following themes emerged from my analysis of the free-text answers provided by the survey participants. These themes and topics help to address the following questions: What is it about music artist management business structures, industry trends and developments in wider cultural life in Australia and overseas that are driving these challenges? How can music artist managers and their teams respond to them?

The themes that emerged included the challenge of breaking emerging artists, balancing costs and income, navigating the demands of digital technologies and the increased workload associated with this, maintaining mental and physical health, dealing with a lack of commercial success, dealing with lawyers, obtaining live performance opportunities for clients, maintaining motivation and finding staff and structural solutions that help music artists and managers realise their visions.

Of these themes, the two that were most frequently discussed were 'navigating the digital era' and 'balancing costs and income'. Two illustrative quotations concerning the increased workload placed on music artist managers in the digital era follow:

Artist managers have a huge role to play in developing their artists digitally—and it's very overwhelming. Suddenly, artist managers play a more involved role than has ever been the case—we are social/digital managers, content creators (with our artists), and so much more. It's tricky and stressful, thankless and is work we aren't ever able to be prepared for. This is largely because there is no correct way to work in the 21st century and everything rests on our luck with the algorithm.

> Digital marketing is a specialist area, and way too much of artists' and management time is used (unpaid) in this space. Partners need to tool up in this area.
>
> (Survey)

Some representative quotations from the 'costs versus income' theme are as follows. For some of the participants, the most significant challenges for their sustainability as artist managers in the next five years were the following:

> Earning enough money to grow. The ability to earn a living wage, stability in touring nationally and internationally. Balancing income of the business as costs continue to rise.
>
> > Cost of overseas exploitation and touring.
> > Low income potential and high workload.
>
> (Survey)

Of course, it is difficult to sustain a living as a music artist manager partly because it is hard to sustain one as a music artist. One participant noted:

> It's hard to see opportunity. It feels like it's just getting harder and my dream of being a full-time artist manager slips through my fingers a little more each year as it becomes harder and harder for artists to make a liveable wage. Costs of touring and costs of living are increasing and yet it's hard to drive an increase to ticket prices or performance fees. Physical merch sales are dwindling, which makes it hard to diversify income streams and digital streaming income is basically a joke.
>
> (Survey)

The participants suggested potential solutions to these challenges including managers being paid an hourly rate and/or music artist managers being given master points on each record their music artist client releases, and some small publishing share on each co-write, enabling them to have equity in the business they are building:

> In a DIY world, I believe artist managers will become artist consultants, paid an hourly rate on fixed-term contract rather than long-term commissions.

> A larger share of recorded music revenue relative to artist managers' influence in the creation, marketing and distribution of recorded music. IP [intellectual property] rights for works created during a manager's term in perpetuity. Employment opportunities in adjacent industries where music management skills are transferable (sport for example).
>
> (Survey)

The free-text answers in the survey manifested a paradox; the participants clearly felt that music artist managers were 'extremely undervalued/poorly remunerated' but that they have also 'never been more important'.

The role of music lawyers

So how have music artist managers reached this point? Surely this is a serious problem for the music business overall as an industrial ecosystem of many small enterprises that lack the human resources infrastructure of larger, more corporatised sectors? As indicated earlier, 81 per cent of participants stated that they believed there should be changes in management agreements with music artists. While there were only two comments concerning lawyers in the survey, along with a perception that there is a lack of streaming revenue for Australian artists, the following participant alluded to the contribution they perceive music lawyers make to the problems outlined earlier:

> The biggest issue in the Australian market is the music lawyers. Half of them are also managers, which is an incredible conflict of interest, and they are doing a disservice to managers and our wider industry. Streaming is also a big issue in Australia. Consumption of Australian artists' [music is] decreasing at a rapid rate. Labels are signing less as they're losing money and are also being taken advantage of by the lawyers.
>
> (Survey)

In response to the question of how the AAM could support managers with some of these challenges, one participant said: 'Government lobbying for grants and tax offsets, and also lobbying of the major legal firms. We should also consider whether or not lawyers are also allowed to be managers' (Survey).

While it would not be possible to prohibit lawyers from also becoming music artist managers because no formal qualification is required—anyone can become an artist manager—I interpret this comment to mean that, for this participant, consideration needs to be given to the role lawyers play, intentionally or otherwise, in impeding change in music artist managers' financial structures/agreements despite managers now having more responsibilities. Further, while there have been various attempts to regulate artist managers (see Gilenson, 1990; Hertz, 1988; Morrow, 2013), these attempts have been driven primarily by lawyers. In this chapter I take a different approach because there is a need to consider the contribution lawyers make to the problems discussed in this book, and there may be a blind spot, so to speak, when lawyers themselves attempt to resolve them.

Broad norms

In terms of research design, the broad-based survey that generated the quantitative data and the relatively short free-text responses outlined earlier was followed by methods that generated more in-depth responses. These included interviews and focus groups that picked up on the key themes raised by the survey. Following the 2022 survey, in 2023, I interviewed 17 participants and conducted two focus groups. The interviews and focus groups enabled me to engage with the participants in often-lengthy discussion of the key issues.

In response to the negative survey comments concerning the problematic role music lawyers play in the field, I deemed it necessary to interview some lawyers and give them a right of reply. What emerged from this process was a paradox; when it comes to artist management agreements, some of the participants who are managers said that there are broad norms or standards, while others, particularly the music lawyers, argued that there are no industry standards; the terms of such agreements depend on context, the market decides the terms not the lawyers and therefore set standards do not exist.

This paradox represents a significant problem. Discussing what he called new realism in 'strategic' reward management, Brown (2019) engaged with the work of Oliver (1997) in a discussion of 'the influence of unwritten but powerful industry norms of practice' (p. 58). He noted that these norms encourage what Arrowsmith and Sissons (1999) termed 'sectoral convoys' (as cited in Brown, 2019, p. 58). What is meant by sectoral convoy here is that this distinct part of the music business continues to move together like a group of vehicles that travel together for mutual support and protection. This is a useful metaphor for considering reward management in music artist management; the influence of powerful but unwritten industry norms is leading some managers to believe that lawyers have a role in forcing historic practices onto them as they walk like zombies into the future. Clearly there is a perception among managers that the sector does travel together in this regard; however, rather than doing so for mutual support and protection, it is competition between managers within the 'convoy' which is leading them to agree to what are, from their perspective, unsustainable management agreements. Regarding the so-called industry standard, Australian artist manager and current AAM Co-Chair Jess Keeley noted on the BIGSOUND panel in 2022 that:

> I always think we inherit what's been done 10 years before, 20 years, or 50 years before and then we repeat, and repeat and repeat and everything changes around us, except for that conversation . . . it's a really significant self-driven job . . . when you're walking into a relationship with someone, and you're a very early manager, early artist or manager, neither of you has reference points. So, this is why that industry standard becomes ubiquitous . . . it just could be something you Google . . . [and] there's no

framework where we're able to be, I suppose, more fluid and more adventurous with it, because it's a really intimidating industry to go into.

(Dawson et al., 2022)

The perception among managers, particularly entry-level ones, that there are broad norms or industry standards is significant. Rather than proactively aligning rewards for managers with the strategic and performance requirements of the artist's business, the lack of a framework for alternative models leads to a process of simply tweaking historic practices—only when necessary—and copying what competitors do, or agreeing to terms because there is a perception that they are those a competitor has. In the absence of a framework for alternative and more contemporary models, the patterns of reward management risk being stuck in outdated norms. One artist manager who participated in this research explained:

> These deals have stagnated despite changing conditions around the relationship of an artist and a manager. Lawyers referring to standards, or [saying] 'It's not standard', is actually one of the reasons why deals have remained as they were in the 1980s, despite social media, and despite all this additional labour placed on managers and with no label to help in many instances. . . . Look, professional advisors are needed, but using terminology like 'standard terms' in relation to management agreements is actually not helpful. Because practically, there are no standard terms. When it comes to artists' management agreements, there is a spectrum of terms, some are more acceptable than others, and some are probably more universally used than others. And that is the key difference.

(Interview 6)

While this manager did argue that lawyers can be unhelpful in this way, ultimately lawyers are professional advisors to artists, who make the final decision. However, artists are often young and inexperienced and may lack the confidence to pursue more innovative solutions when it comes to management agreements. They search for reference points and cling to the safety of what they think of as standard terms. They bring these anxieties to management agreement negotiations while also being understandably self-interested.

Artists are unlikely to be convinced by arguments like those Adam Smith (1776/1982) made in his publication *The wealth of nations*, that an increase in the profits of private entrepreneurs such as managers in the music business will be the basis for an increase in collective wealth and prosperity in the music business overall. The argument that better reward management would benefit businesses overall is a challenging one to make because many individual artists are not interested in the wider strategic objective of better reward management practices for managers. They are primarily focused on their own financial rewards relative to what they pay out to their managers. The key task for managers is to be better at 'selling' to their artist clients their ability to add value. While artists are the ultimate decision makers here, the participant cited earlier argued that lawyers are stakeholders in the deal-making process:

> I think that we need to accept more generally and more broadly that we are open to broader negotiations with more creativity and originality within the structure of deals that pertain more to the work and the labour that artist managers now invest into an artist from a very early point, particularly where they might not be benefiting for some years from direct income. That discussion needs to be had openly and honestly. But that discussion also needs to include all the stakeholders that are involved in making those deals . . . that would be a trilogy, the manager, the artist and the legal representation.
>
> (Interview 6)

Interestingly, the lawyers I interviewed made comments that resonated with this manager's perspective on agreements. One participant, who is a senior Australian music lawyer, noted that managers do not have to

> do it one way or another. It's an arm's-length commercial negotiation. You have to decide what you think is appropriate and you have to explain that to the artist and sell it. Managers often complain and say 'Argh, it's stacked against me. Lawyers won't agree it', or, you know, 'Artists won't agree it, it's the norms.' It's like well, yes, there are broad norms that people, in a broad sense, will say, 'Well, I've asked my friends. I've asked my lawyer. I've asked other people in this business. They say that's not usual.' But it depends on what you're asking as to how usual or unusual it is, and it depends on what the value proposition is.
>
> (Interview 10)

Another senior music lawyer I interviewed, David Vodicka, implied that artists' strategic objectives can and are being realised through management agreements—that is, it is possible to design 'tailored reward policies to suit their strategy, rather than simply copying general market and sector practice' (Brown, 2019, p. 66). Vodicka noted:

> My opinion about that isn't so much whether I think anything's right or wrong. I think ultimately, people make the mistake and assumption that these things are set in stone; they're not. They haven't been around for that long and really, all these things is an agreement between two parties that has to be negotiated. And the parties have to figure out what it is that they think is acceptable for them . . . whenever I'm asked these questions, I find it interesting. Because ultimately . . . there are no rules

for management agreements. People can make whatever arrangement that
they want. The difficulty I find for managers is adequately selling themselves to the artists to explain why they want that.

(Interview 16)

The problem here, according to David Vodicka, is that managers need to better articulate the value they bring to the relationship to artists as the ultimate
decision makers and better outline the vision they have for the artist's business
relative to their proposed terms.

Yet, particularly at the entry level, the issue here seems to be caused by
managers and artists searching for reference points regarding the 'industry
standards' that are frequently discussed when in fact there are no such singular
reference points. Problematically, in the following example, David Vodicka
stated that he would not disclose that there are no standards to the parties he
is advising:

I feel that lawyers are not the gatekeepers. But if someone rings and goes,
'Is this standard?' You know, like, the amount of times I have this question—I would never say this to people—but you just go, 'Fellas [sic], there
is no standard. It is an agreement.'

(Interview 16)

Clearly there is a range of terms for management agreements and scope for
further innovation in what is agreed between an artist and a manager; there
technically are no standards—it simply depends on what is agreed between
the two parties. Yet there is equally clearly a strong perception of permanence
regarding the terms of agreements amongst many of the artist managers who
participated. Senior Australian artist manager John Watson described this as
an 'illusion of permanence':

As with many things in life, there is the illusion of permanence—what we
perceive as norms were in their time abnormal. And there were norms that
existed before them. So, the norms that existed before them—which I'm
not advocating that we return to, they were very unfair to artists—but they
put the manager in the middle of things. Artists tended to sign to managers' production companies, and then be signed on from that. So that meant,
in the 60s, it was very common for Andrew Loog Oldham to own all the
Rolling Stones masters until he screwed up and accidentally gave them all
to Allen Klein. . . . Springsteen's first deal with Mike Appel—appalling
deal, wouldn't recommend it under any circumstances to anyone. But the
point is, the idea of managers working on a services basis is something that
became the norm in the late 70s, early 80s, along with recoupable recording deals that involved getting big recording advances. Artists before that
never had recoupable advances. The Beatles' record deal was a penny a

record, regardless of their recording costs. Abbey Road was free to them, in a way. So, the fact that something looks permanent, doesn't mean that it is permanent, the building behind you will one day be dust.

(Interview 13)

The 'broad norm' prior to the 1970s was for music artist managers to operate more like film producers do, with their production company owning the master copyright in the artist's recordings. Towse (2019, p. 501) noted that in the film industry, along with the film director, in some countries the film producer also obtains authors' rights. In the 1960s managers such as Andrew Loog Oldham and Mike Appel were also record producers and thus operated in a similar way.

A further rationalisation of the changes post circa 1970 was provided by the following focus group participant and concerns poor management behaviour in the past. This participant discussed the difficulties of

trying to find a new model that isn't just purely a reactive one when [the standard] is based upon bad situations that have happened in the past, which I think is how the management deals are landed into, the rough standard position that you find in Australia is a result of bad managers, or bad artists who have behaved badly. And people have had to put safeguards in that inherently limit the scope of what the agreements can do. It'd be nice if we can wipe the slate clean and start again. But unfortunately, a lot of those historical events . . . do colour our ability to change these kinds of things. If I'm going to go and ask an artist for perpetual rights on things, I'm going to get pushback on that from a lawyer. Because I've been in this situation where they go, 'Oh, well, let me tell you about artist x, they had this manager for five minutes.' They've now tainted perpetual rights. For me, being questioned even on fairly minor changes, or incremental changes to the current position, does make it hard as a manager to see a pathway forward as to how more radical change could be realised.

(Focus Group 2)

Unfortunately, past events in this way do limit a manager's attempts to put their case for alternative ways management agreements could be structured, and more recent events in Australia do not help. For example, Australian pop artist Guy Sebastian's former manager Titus Day was jailed in November 2022 for embezzling AUD 600,000 from Sebastian (Wells, 2022). This type of event affects artist management agreement negotiations generally. This can lead to managers being poorly remunerated while being given a lot more responsibility, which can put them under immense stress and pressure. Their wellbeing can also be further impacted because at the same time they are villainised by music artists. This clearly impacts the motivation and mental health of some of the music artist managers who participated in the survey. The following short-answer text responses concern the challenges music artist managers face:

> Look it's not a job I'd recommend to anyone. For the most part managers are overworked, underpaid and then vilified by musicians so it's lose, lose, lose. I don't know why I'm still doing it tbh [to be honest].

> I think we have become the most essential part of the industry at the moment yet also the most unappreciated. There is opportunity for growth and change but only if the lack of appreciating is recognised by both artists and industry players, and by more than lip service.
>
> (Survey)

A key finding here therefore is that artists and artist managers need to better understand that there are no norms[1]—there is only the market for their services—and one of the solutions here simply involves them being able to better articulate their value in a competitive environment, as well as the ethical standards they will bring to the role. Artist manager John Watson noted: 'I wouldn't disagree with the proposition that management agreements are framed as they are to protect artists from management malfeasance . . . and I wouldn't disagree that such protection is warranted'. However, he also noted that 'if someone said—just for example—that managers can't ever get points in perpetuity like a producer gets points in perpetuity then I would say that's an arbitrary choice and it may well change as managers become increasingly fundamental' (Interview 13). This suggests that the argument that the difference between management agreements and producer agreements is arbitrary could be used by managers in negotiations. This could help managers address the perception that management agreements are structured the way they are to limit the risk to artists of poor manager behaviour. Lawyers representing artists can obviously provide numerous examples of past bad behaviour by managers. My argument in relation to this is that the risks to artists of future poor manager behaviour need to be balanced against the benefits that more strategic reward management could bring.

This is important because, as Chaparro and Musgrave (2021) argued, 'cultural (as opposed to regulatory) change can help guide and inform managerial decision-making' (p. 1). As I argued in Chapter 2, leadership in the relationship between an artist and their manager works both ways. This means that managers have a duty of care to artists, but artists also have a duty of care to managers. Following the tragic death of Avicii (Tim Bergling) in 2018, Chaparro and Musgrave noted that many media commentators as well as Bergling's own family asked whether

> questions vis-à-vis the role and responsibilities of music managers to protect the mental and physical health of musicians . . . and questions around

the potentially exploitative nature of their contractual arrangements had been present in the case of Avicii's manager for several years prior.

(p. 2)

The argument here is that there was a failure in a key aspect of how this artist was led by their manager, in particular an allegation that the manager failed to exercise their duty of care. Though the question could also be asked whether there was failure in how the manager was led by way of the management agreement that was signed in the first instance. A by-product of the short-termism of some artist management agreements is that some managers, such as Avicii's manager Arash Pournouri, may allegedly have contributed to overworking the artist, and this may have undermined the artist's wellbeing. This is a significant by-product: agreements that are designed to protect artists and limit their risk may actually be causing them harm if by design they incentivise the short-term interests of the manager.

To change this situation, collective action among managers is needed. The AAM as an association is an attempt at collective action by managers. In a sense, therefore, the negotiations required to change these agreements are trilateral: 1) the artist (and their lawyer), 2) the manager and 3) AAM (representing the collective will of mangers). Managers, however, even when working in a collective-action body like the AMM, remain competitors. The key question is, then, would collective action bring managers more utility than exploiting any individual advantages they may have? This is the classic dilemma of collective action.

Music artist management value propositions

Rather than reinforcing the perception of some managers that there are broad norms, the lawyers who participated highlighted that there are many different types of agreements being used in the field. This diversity in the terms of management agreements suggests a need for some managers to move away from the illusion of permanence of industry norms to arguing instead for best fit in terms of strategy, goals and the value proposition they bring to the negotiation. When asked about different models, one lawyer who participated said,

> I think it very much depends. It's a value proposition, this stuff. It's a bit like saying, well, what should a record deal look like? You know, what should a producer be paid? It depends. If you're a global hit maker, and you're a producer, you can get a $100,000 US per track. If you're a brand-new producer, you get nothing per track, you're begging to be in the room.
>
> (Interview 10)

The type of agreement depends on the manager's track record. It also depends on the career stage of the artist. This lawyer noted,

> If you want to be managed by TaP, TaP want 25 per cent, not 20. . . . TaP's view is, 'Well, the level of service offering that we have is more than other managers. We've got a bigger team, we do more, we've got more success, and that's what we charge. And if you don't want to be managed by us, that that's totally fine.' And the reality is, people want to be managed by them.
>
> (Interview 10)

There are correlations between strategic business typologies and the type of agreement managers can realise in the music business. In terms of Miles and Snow's (Miles & Snow, 2003; Miles et al., 1978) business strategy typology, artists pursuing a 'prospector' strategy of innovation, because their music is yet to find a large audience, are more likely to agree to favourable terms for their manager. Artists using a 'defender' strategy because they already have a large audience can offer less favourable terms. Australian artist manager Jess Keeley noted on the BIGSOUND panel in 2022 that

> it really depends on the scale of what you're working with. So, if you're talking to an artist and you're developing them from a really early stage, they probably think that [the 20 per cent model] is okay. Like it's an initial conversation. It's going to be developmental. And then when you speak to an artist about a 20 per cent model, and they're making AUD 3 million a year, that seems gratuitous for them, that seems like an excessive amount of money to be paid to a manager.
>
> (Dawson et al., 2022)

The market position of both the manager and the artist are factors here. Rather than discussing an 'industry standard' that does not exist, managers should argue for best fit in terms of both their and the artist's positioning. Senior Australian music lawyer David Vodicka noted that

> managers need to be able to sustain the argument and make a cogent and persuasive argument to artists. Lawyers don't make the rules . . . our firm would represent a vast majority of the artists in this market . . . we do obviously see a ton of management agreements . . . we've gone through and re-done our own base template for management companies, which is manager-biased, right, and we put a whole lot of variables in it, but a lot of established managers take no effort in their agreements, and they actually just recycle old agreements. The amount of times that I have seen other lawyers use our template agreements, which we've spent time, effort and money on, is quite surprising, to the point where people haven't removed

my name from the document. And I feel that creating agreements, and arguing these things out, requires a degree of investment. And often managers are not in a position or don't want to spend anything, in terms of doing that . . . for change to be effective, you need to be able to convince people.

(Interview 16)

Therefore, while some of the managers cited earlier argued that lawyers are part of the problem, this lawyer in turn argued that managers are similarly implicated in the problems facing the industry. And of course, while there may be a perception amongst the music artist manager community that lawyers are part of the problem, lawyers are also part of the solution for managers who desire more progressive management agreements—music lawyers also represent managers in negotiations. David Vodicka posited,

I would 100 per cent agree when representing managers—and we do represent managers—that it's a fundamentally different industry from what it was 10 to 15 years ago, in terms of income streams. And if you're just talking about record income, for example, or the way that revenue is now generated for artists, having a three-year post-term commission for the amount of time and effort you invest in an artist, to me, makes no sense as a business. If you used to get all your money in pretty much three years after your term was done, because it was CD sales, or vinyl or whatever, and it was a big, number-one record, and then if you're huge it leaks out for a few years, I get it. But the fact of the matter is now if you have a billion-streaming track, that is going to keep earning money for a considerable period of time. . . . I never get asked these questions by managers, seriously. All I hear are complaints. I go, 'Fellas [sic], you've got to make your own way.' You've got to put yourself forward and basically convince people. . . . But to me, it's pretty obvious that you should be getting a longer post-term commission.

(Interview 16)

These comments suggest that there is a lack of investment in the development of agreement templates by managers and context-appropriate arguments being put by them in many artist management agreement negotiations, and this is leading to low levels of artist, and other stakeholder, understanding of reward strategies, practices and processes that better reflect contemporary realities.

So, are managers' views being neglected by artists and their lawyers in making reward decisions, or are managers simply not articulating them well enough, or at all? Lawyers represent both sides of management agreement negotiations, and the ones I interviewed are open to helping managers and artists understand and reach more appropriate agreements. They can help managers to make clearer and more convincing arguments to artists. Similar to David Vodicka's arguments, the following senior music lawyer also agreed that the context has changed:

> The environment has changed and a lot of the time it's absolutely in the artist's interest not to be signing record deals and to put out records themselves or do it on services deals . . . and in those instances the managers do a lot more work and the value comes a lot later down the path. So, if you, say, do a deal with, let's say it's The Orchard, and they're going to put out the album and they're going to front $100,000 towards the marketing costs, you might get 70 per cent[2] on the back end on that for three or four years, and after that you get 100 per cent. So, if you're doing that record deal in year one, you've got a lot more work to do because the label's [The Orchard] not going to do the same things that a traditional record label is going to do. . . . It's a lot more work for the manager and the income comes a lot later, but the income is a lot more for a lot longer. So, for a manager to say 'Hey, I'm very supportive of us going down this path, not signing it to a frontline label like Sony, Warner, Universal, but doing something on a services deal where, in the long run, you'll make way more money and you'll own your own copyright. But the trade-off is we won't make money for longer, I want to have my deal with you reflect that that's what we're doing.
>
> (Interview 10)

The type of agreement negotiated in this scenario will look quite different to the one outlined in Chapter 1. The terms outlined in Chapter 1 are, according to the music lawyer cited earlier, derivative of the 'the classic US manager model' (Interview 10), whereby

> American managers, mostly, will say, 'Yeah, I'll manage you. I'm going to spend three months, go out and put it out to everyone I can, get an attorney on board, put it out for deals, and if we get a big pub [song publishing] deal and a big record deal, I'm going to take my cut of that. That gets me some payday off the bat. They're going to do all the work. I'm going to put all the work back on the label and on the publisher. My job is to be like, "Do your job!" I'm not going to do too much more, and if it works, I'll make my commissions on touring.'
>
> (Interview 10)

A mismatch occurs when a management agreement that is designed for this type of approach,[3] which involves the agreement working alongside the agreements that an artist signs with a very active record label and a proactive song publisher, is applied to the scenario outlined earlier whereby the artist self-releases their music.

But of course, it may not be clear at the outset whether the artist will sign directly to a major label and a major song publisher. For example, they might change direction, strategically self-releasing instead of signing directly to a major label as originally planned, or simply because there is no other option because the label has no interest. Managers may also have difficulties articulating their value proposition in words during a management agreement negotiation, and, according to this music lawyer, they may be better off attempting to demonstrate the value they bring through action:

> If you're an intelligent manager . . . in that situation, where you are competing with people [to sign an artist], and you don't have a relationship yet, you've got to get in there and build a relationship and prove it and then revisit it, I'd say. You'd say, 'You know what, I'm going to explain this to you upfront. Let's agree more regular terms if that's what the bugbear is. . . . Let's get going. But I want to sit down with you guys in six months and have a chat about how we structure this, and why and what the impact is for us, what the service level is I will provide. And if you agree, we should re-skin it'. . . . I think the idea that off the bat that artists are just going to say to managers 'Here's all this stuff'. It's not such an easy thing to ask if you're not a proven manager . . . if you're a proven manager that the artist desperately wants to be managed by, then you can ask anything you like, within reason.
>
> (Interview 10)

As I outlined in Chapter 1, a point of tension when it comes to management agreements concerns the post-term commission rates. Some managers who participated were hesitant to present a clause in an agreement that involves post-term participation in the income that is longer than three to five years because the artist and their lawyer would never agree to it:

> We had advice from an Australian lawyer [regarding] our new management template that we're doing for self-released music or in self-released territories [that we should] have 20-year post terms, that's what we're trying to do, and it makes a lot of sense. But I laugh at it, because I'm pretty sure that it's great in theory, but if we came up against the same lawyer and pitched that to an artist they were representing, they would just be like, 'absolutely not'.
>
> (Focus Group 1)

However, remuneration structures and systems are influenced by the context and culture in which they are implemented and the power relations that exist (White & Druker, 2008), and interestingly the lawyer cited earlier is willing to advise artists to agree to longer post-termination commission rates when it comes to artists that they manage alongside their work as a lawyer:

> My management deal with the acts that I manage is that I have no committed term. They can end it at will at any time. But the things that I've

worked on with them, I'm commissioning in perpetuity because we've built something DIY [do it yourself] from the ground up. I've let them put every dollar that we make back into it. I'm basically varying commissions ad infinitum, in a sense, for a while, because I'm building them something they're going to own forever and they're going to do so much better out of our setup than they would if we went and signed it somewhere else, which a less experienced operative would have done.

(Interview 10)

In contrast to the argument from the survey (cited at the top of this chapter) that the management community should question whether lawyers should also be allowed to be managers, this music lawyer argued the opposite: being involved in different roles across the industry enables stakeholders such as lawyers to have empathy for the different parties' interests in negotiations:

It's easy for someone to go, 'Argh, artists shouldn't complain, rah, rah.' But when you've worn the artist hat and you've spent a year on the road on tour playing shitty gigs all over regional Australia, you're like, 'No, I understand that point of view, like I understand what goes into it, I know what it's like spending lots of time in a shitty bus with lots of people . . . ' Then there's the highs and lows of excitement of deal time, and then, when the thing goes cold, and no one is listening. . . . I think all that stuff is really relevant and important. . . . At the same time, the roller coaster of management, I understand it. I understand what the job entails. I understand the boundarylessness of it, that there is an unlimited amount of hours you could spend doing the job. . . . I think the more you understand the business, the more able you are to understand it from everyone's point of view and help people come to a sensible resolution.

(Interview 10)

For this lawyer, having empathy for the different stakeholders' points of view is key to helping the parties navigate their way to appropriate agreements.

Linear to circular career development

Understanding broader paradigm shifts relating to how careers develop in the music business is important as well. In an earlier book I co-wrote (Hughes et al., 2016), we argued that within what we called 'the new music industries' there has been a paradigm shift from linear career development to circular career development for artists. The type of management agreements outlined in Chapter 1, and the type of agreement described earlier as the US manager model, were originally designed for the traditional linear process. This process involved the artist finding a manager who had pre-existing relationships with entities such as record labels, song publishers and booking agents. If these entities signed the artist, then the people working for them would help expose the artist to audiences by booking them into live performance opportunities, making their music available at record stores, in film and TV by way of synchronisation agreements, and by promoting their music through media outlets, etc. The artist's music would then be available at the end of this process on a relatively short list of available music from which audiences could choose. This was described as linear because the various transactions occurred in this order: 'artist—industry person—industry person—industry person—fan' (p. 28).

The trend toward artists self-releasing music, which was discussed earlier, has arisen due to the contemporary, more circular model of career development. This model has emerged simply because the artist is now able to communicate directly with their audience. If the artist can engage enough of an audience directly, then the artist has a choice; they can either self-release their music to this growing audience or come to an agreement with other industry stakeholders who are in turn reacting to these direct connections and who are interested in helping grow the artist's career further. This is described as circular because the transactions involved occur in this order: 'artist—fan—industry—artist' (p. 28). This is a circle because it begins with the direct artist-audience communication and circles back to this over and over in a way that is informed by the principles of agile project management (see Morrow, 2018). In this sense, record labels, song publishers, booking agents, the media and other stakeholders have become more reactive to direct artist-audience connections. In the foreword to our 2016 book, Australian artist manager John Watson described this situation as follows:

> We thus live in a world of 'build it and they will come', with the still-coveted high rotation radio spins and magazine covers increasingly going to artists who have already proved online that their creations are made of the right stuff. This is bad news for anyone sitting around hoping some Svengali will swoop out of the clouds and make them a star, but it is fantastic news for hard-working artists who are keen to engage directly with their audience. It's also good news for music consumers who have more access to more music, more affordably than ever, but it's mixed news for the people who used to be gatekeepers.
>
> (in Hughes et al., 2016, p. viii)

The type of artist management agreements outlined in Chapter 1 were designed for the linear process rather than the circular one. The circular model requires more labour from managers for several reasons. First, there is the work involved in connecting directly with audiences in the first instance, either to attract investors or to work towards self-releasing. Second, if the artist connects with an audience and then decides to self-release, then the 'industry person' in the circle becomes the manager along with the artist because self-releasing usually involves the manager's labour and the artist's capital.

A problem with this linear-circular binary, though, is that it creates the perception that artists have a choice as to whether they pursue a linear or circular approach. This is a false perception because, even if a label becomes involved nowadays, the artist still often needs to connect directly with their audience, and this needs to be managed and led in an ongoing way. Further, to attract labels in the first instance, the artist must demonstrate that they have direct connections with their audience and that the number of these connections is growing exponentially as evidenced by the data—not just having the potential to grow. Therefore, in the 'new music industries' there is now simply a spectrum of circular career development models; the linear model outlined earlier for the most part simply does not exist anymore. This is why the type of artist management agreements outlined in Chapter 1 were described by many participants in my study as not reflecting the current processes.

Circle of control/circle of influence

So far, this chapter has focused on artist management agreements and the tension between managers and lawyers when it comes to forming these agreements. However, in addition to these agreements, there are other issues and challenges that managers face in the music business stemming from the broader context in which they operate. The reason for focusing on agreements in the first instance is that the negotiation of these agreements is arguably within a manager's circle of control/locus of control (Lefcourt, 1992; Rotter, 1990). Managers can put their case and argue for different terms in their agreements, or for new business models entirely.

Many of the other issues and challenges that arose in the research data lie outside managers' circle of control, instead either residing in their circle of influence, or simply being out of their control or influence entirely. Some of these other issues directly relate to the type of management agreements outlined in Chapter 1 being out of date, such as a perceived exit strategy problem: 'If I start a business and run a business for 20 years, then I'm building something . . . like any business, you're building for an exit strategy. . . . I have no business to sell like that' (Interview 7). There is also a perception that less skilled management time is being invested in emerging artists: 'Senior managers just aren't signing new and emerging artists because the last couple of years have just made them realise they don't want to work for free for that long anymore' (Interview 9). However, there are other issues such as the perceived exodus of talented managers from the business that are only partly related to management agreements being out of date because there are several other issues beyond a manager's control that are also causing this exodus. Discussing the perceived exodus of managers, one participant said: 'The management model is archaic. It's broken, doesn't work. We're seeing a mass exodus of managers globally, get out of the game, and that's a huge blow' (Focus Group 1).

While another posited that

> managers often leave the industry and go into other pockets of the music industry or elsewhere, which is where I'd say over half of the managers that I knew 10 years ago, probably 70 to 75 per cent are not managers anymore, because the business is not stable. It's hugely based on luck and so you have this massive brain drain.
>
> (Interview 14)

The point made here—that a manager's success and staying power in the business is largely based on luck—suggests that, while the perceived exodus of managers may in part be related to the issues with management agreements outlined earlier, luck is at play here too simply because there are not enough highly successful artists in the Australian music business to manage and too many managers. For example, discussing the perceived exodus of managers, one participant noted,

> To be fair, the first reason is that, for every 1000 artists who try to do this, there might be half a dozen who have careers that could actually be sustainable for artists and managers. So, it's a very speculative thing to do . . . it's a difficult thing to be in for a long time.
>
> (Interview 1)

Other participants discussed the issue of the age of managers and observed that the number of managers over the age of 30 drops off dramatically:

> The pool of managers out there aged between 20ish and 30 is large. The pool of managers after 30 is very small because there's a huge attrition rate. . . . It's probably akin to being talent in lots of ways where there's an awful lot of artists out there aged between 20 and 30, there's not a lot of artists that are out there post-30 that are pursuing full-time careers. Because there's a phase of life where you're like, 'I'm happy to take these risks. I'll hate myself if I don't. I don't want to look back and go "I could have been that manager, I could've been that person. I want to do those things. I think I've got what it takes, I think I've got the ability to pick talent. I've got the ability to do that stuff."' And after a while, either it happens, and it can happen because you do have that talent. But it can also happen because you get lucky, and vice versa, you can have all the talent and things just don't go your way.
>
> (Interview 10)

While luck can be within a manager's circle of influence because they set themselves up to be lucky—'You were out there doing the right things, doing everything that you can, walking down the street so that when luck bumped into you, you thought, "that was lucky," but no, you were there on the street'

(George Stein, as cited in Morrow, 2006, p. 340)—a number of other issues discussed in the interviews and focus groups relating to the perceived exodus of managers are outside managers' control or influence. These include music no longer being as central to youth activity; the challenge of achieving sustainability in a small market such as Australia; there being no 'middle class' of artists in Australia; education and training not making it to the coalface; the threat of artificial intelligence; and music artist management being a male-dominated profession, one that also lacks diversity generally. Further, the management role was described as fulfilling a shock-absorber function, and this means that the role itself is innately stressful, often leading to burnout and subsequent attrition. Artist manager John Watson put it this way:

> Another way of conceptualising the management role is like a shock absorber . . . between the artist and the industry. The artist has a certain set of expectations about what the world should be delivering to them: the headlining spot on the festival, the high rotation add on the radio station. The industry has a certain set of expectations, or a certain set of needs for the artists: to come and play this show for free. One of your roles is to mediate that exchange. So, the challenge is when you have very bad alignment between those things. So, the artist expects to be headlining the festival, the festival doesn't even think they should be on the bill . . . trying to be that shock absorber can be very, very difficult.
>
> (Interview 13)

This challenge of fulfilling a shock absorber function is compounded by the need to manage public perceptions of an artist and mask any difficulties they may be having. Waston continued,

> Your job is to always make the artists seem magical, to make it seem like their work is levitating and otherworldly . . . if you ask a manager how their artist is going, they'll go, 'They are amazing, they're white hot, I cannot believe how great they are', when in fact they're backstage right now having a punch up. So, one of the great stresses of the job is constantly having to do jazz hands around how good things are and having no outlet for that.
>
> (Interview 13)

Watson also framed the innate stress in the role in the following way:

> Half of the role is outward looking to the industry and half is inward looking to the artist. The perception is that the manager spends their time largely on the outward-looking stuff, generating the opportunities, landing the deals, maximising the business stuff. In truth, with many artists you actually spend the majority of your time trying to stop them from shooting themselves in the foot in various ways. And that process of stopping the

band from squabbling or breaking up, stopping the band from making a really poor decision, stopping the band from pushing into doing something they really shouldn't do, etc. is stressful for a whole bunch of reasons.

(Interview 13)

These inherent stresses of the role are outside of the manager's control or influence—the role is what it is. All managers can do is mitigate this stress by taking part in emotional resilience training and the like.

Another issue managers face that is in some ways within their control and influence, and in other ways well outside of it, is the artist's business model. Joel Connolly, a former Australian music artist manager who now works for Australian venture capital company Blackbird as creative director, argued that the music business stifles creativity and denies artists their agency (Connolly, 2021). He noted that artists/bands and their managers create a lot of value but they themselves only capture a small amount of this value. Similarly, Giblin and Doctorow (2022) argued that we are in a new era of what they call 'chokepoint capitalism' whereby big tech, big content and big media create barriers to competition, what US investor Warren Buffett calls 'moats', that enable them to capture value that would otherwise go to others such as artists/bands—and their managers.

For Connolly (2021), having a direct relationship with customers (in our case, music fans) is the most fundamental rule for creating a great business. For him, the music business, at many different points, attempts to stop artists from having such direct relationships. For example, there is a perception that the circular career development model outlined earlier involves direct connections between an artist and their audience, but what is actually happening is that platforms such as Spotify, Apple Music, Facebook, Instagram, TikTok, etc. only enable artists to have indirect relationships with their audience through their platforms. Connolly pointed out that

> Spotify and Apple will never tell you who is listening to your music. They will never tell you who is paying for it. They barely tell you how they are listening to it or when . . . they will never give you their email addresses or allow you to contact them off-platform.

Connolly pointed out that many artists do not even know this is happening. This not only occurs through social media platforms but also when it comes to live music ticket sales.

This is something that Rowan Brand and I experienced when we were co-managing the Australian band Boy & Bear. Using ecommerce platform Music Glue's services, we attempted to obtain an allocation of tickets for the band's shows at venues such as the Enmore in Sydney and the Forum in Melbourne so that the band could sell these directly to their fans and thus retain the data and build and manage their own direct relationship with their audience. Suffice to say that there was immense pushback on our attempts from live music agents, venue bookers, promoters and venues, to the extent that we were often denied any allocation, or if the band were allocated some tickets to sell directly, the number of tickets was small.

Giblin and Doctorow's (2022) theory of chokepoint capitalism has resonance here as this trend towards denying small businesses direct relationships with their customers extends well beyond the music business to many different facets of the modern economy. Chokepoint capitalist models are widespread and are the result of decades-long trends towards both monopolies (where sellers have power over buyers) and monopsonies (where buyers have power over sellers), with Amazon being a prime example of the latter. The arguments put in this chapter—that the type of management agreements outlined in Chapter 1 are unsustainable and that there is a problematic exodus of managers from the business—need to be put into this broader context. If multinational live music corporations such as Live Nation are using what Giblin and Doctorow term 'the anti-competitive flywheel' (p. 9) to eliminate competition in order to capture the lion's share of value that artists create, it is little wonder that music artist managers are feeling the squeeze.

Conclusion

This chapter discussed the issues and challenges that music artist managers face, primarily focusing on artist management agreements. These agreements are at the core of many of the problems this book addresses, and negotiation of these agreements is arguably within a manager's circle of control. The time is right for more managers to put their case and argue (ideally with a collective voice) for different terms in their agreements, or for new business models entirely. Artist manager John Watson argued: 'Ultimately the leverage comes from the perception of artists and lawyers as to who is generating the commercial opportunities' (Interview 13). Record labels, and to a lesser extent song publishers, used to be the dominant source of capital and labour required to build artists' careers by way of the linear career development model discussed in this chapter. This meant that the power was in their hands, and they could agree terms in recording agreements that favoured them.

Many of the research participants discussed the practice of artists self-releasing their music and the spectrum of contemporary circular career development models. Remuneration structures and systems are influenced by the context and culture in which they are implemented and the power relations that exist in these, and with record labels less able to control the business, artists and their managers are doing more for themselves. This can lead to improved recording agreements being offered to artists who have leverage. Alongside these deals, however, managers also need to negotiate improved agreements. It is, though, difficult for managers to obtain the experience and knowledge required to be able to innovate here without, as one of the music lawyers I interviewed said, 'committing yourself to deferring earning a living, because for most managers that is what they do, until they have success. They're living like artists. It's a very similar thing. They sleep on couches when they travel' (Interview 10).

As this chapter uncovered, there are many parallels between music artists and music artist managers, and because there are no rules for management agreements, managers can and should work more like artists and follow music producer Rick Rubin's advice:

> Holding every rule as breakable is a healthy way to live as an artist. It loosens constraints that promote a predictable sameness in our working methods. . . . Any rule is worth testing, be it conscious or unconscious. Challenge your assumptions and methods. You might find a better way.
>
> (Rubin, 2023, pp. 102–103)

Notes

1 I have chosen to use the word 'norms' here over 'standards' because the latter may be codified and thus enforceable. Norms are not usually written and are closer to shared informal community understandings. It seems clear that standards do not exist, but norms do, at least in the minds of many respondents. The responsibility for defining and enforcing standards falls on the AAM. Legislation is arguably too big a hammer. While there have been attempts to license managers in the state of New South Wales (see Morrow, 2013), in most states in Australia management is not a licensed profession and as such the AAM cannot force managers to follow any code of conduct and many managers are not members of the AAM. However, the AAM does 'encourage' compliance with its code of conduct as a condition of membership.
2 In this example the royalty paid to the artist would be 70 per cent for 3 to 4 years, then it would be 100 per cent after this period if the $100,000 advance is recouped by the distributor. This is what is meant by 70 per cent then 100 per cent on the back end.
3 The type of agreements outlined in Chapter 1 arguably assume this type of career development logic.

References

Arrowsmith, J., & Sisson, K. (1999). Pay and Working Time: Towards Organization-based Systems? *British Journal of Industrial Relations, 37*(1), 51–75. https://doi.org/10.1111/1467-8543.00118

Australian Bureau of Statistics (ABS). (2022). *Education and work, Australia.* www.abs.gov.au/statistics/people/education/education-and-work-australia/latest-release

Brown, D. (2019). New realism in 'strategic' reward management: Bringing together research and practice. In S. J. Perkins (Ed.), *The Routledge companion to reward management* (pp. 55–71). Routledge.

Chaparro, G., & Musgrave, G. (2021). Moral music management: Ethical decision-making after Avicii. *International Journal of Music Business Research, 10*(1), 1–14. https://doi.org/10.2478/ijmbr-2021-0001

Connolly, J. (2021, April 12). How the music industry stifles creativity and denies artists their agency. *Meaning Making.* https://joelconnolly.substack.com/p/how-the-music-industry-stifles-creativity

Dawson, O., Keeley, J., & Carey, G. (2022, September 7). *Sustainable relationships? The value of management partnerships* [Panel presentation, G. Morrow, Chair]. BigSound, Brisbane, Queensland.

Giblin, R., & Doctorow, C. (2022). *Chokepoint capitalism: How big tech and big content captured creative labor markets and how we'll win them back.* Scribe Publications.

Gilenson, H. I. (1990). Badlands: Artist—personal manager conflicts of interest in the music industry. *Cardozo Arts & Entertainment Law Journal, 9,* 501–544.

Hertz, B. W. (1988). The regulation of artist representation in the entertainment industry. *Loyola Entertainment Law Journal, 8,* 55–73.

Hughes, D., Evans, M., Morrow, G., & Keith, S. (2016). *The new music industries.* Springer International Publishing. https://doi.org/10.1007/978-3-319-40364-9

Lefcourt, H. M. (1992). Durability and impact of the locus of control construct. *Psychological Bulletin, 112*(3), 411–414. https://doi.org/10.1037/0033-2909.112.3.411

Miles, R. E., & Snow, C. C. (2003). *Organizational strategy, structure, and process.* Stanford University Press.

Miles, R. E., Snow, C. C., Meyer, A. D., & Coleman, H. J. (1978). Organizational strategy, structure, and process. *Academy of Management Review, 3*(3), 546–562. https://doi.org/10.2307/257544

Morrow, G. (2006). *Managerial creativity: A study of artist management practices in the Australian popular music industry* [Doctoral thesis, Macquarie University]. Figshare. https://figshare.mq.edu.au/articles/thesis/Managerial_creativity_a_study_of_artist_management_practices_in_the_Australian_popular_music_industry/19427489

Morrow, G. (2013). Regulating artist managers: An insider's perspective. *International Journal of Music Business Research, 2*(2), 8–35.

Morrow, G. (2018). *Artist management: Agility in the creative and cultural industries.* Routledge.

Morrow, G., & Long, B. (2022). *Association of artist managers: 2022 annual membership survey: Final report.* University of Melbourne. https://doi.org/10.26188/21965786

Oliver, C. (1997). Sustainable competitive advantage: Combining institutional and resource-based views. *Strategic Management Journal, 18*(9), 697–713. https://doi.org/10.1002/(SICI)1097-0266(199710)18:9<697::AID-SMJ909>3.0.CO;2-C

Rotter, J. B. (1990). Internal versus external control of reinforcement: A case history of a variable. *American Psychologist, 45*(4), 489–493. https://doi.org/10.1037/0003-066X.45.4.489

Rubin, R. (2023). *The creative act: A way of being.* Penguin Press.

Smith, A. (1982). *The wealth of nations: Books I—III.* Penguin. (Original work published 1776)

Towse, R. (2019). *A textbook of cultural economics.* Cambridge University Press.

Wells, J. (2022, November 17). Guy Sebastian's former manager jailed for embezzling $600,000 from singer. *ABC News.* www.abc.net.au/news/2022-11-17/guy-sebastian-former-manager-titus-day-jailed-for-four-years/101664154

White, G., & Druker, J. (Eds.). (2008). *Reward management: A critical text* (2nd ed.). Routledge.

4 The ever-expanding role of music artist managers

Introduction

While managers' pay is often ill-defined, the scope of the work they are required to do often is too. As discussed in Chapter 2, the financial reward that an artist pays their manager through the type of agreement outlined in Chapter 1 is unpredictable because it depends on the artist's financial success. Through such an agreement, a manager could earn 15 to 20 per cent of nothing or 15 to 20 per cent of a lot of money. This variable amount remunerates a role with unclear boundaries. The research participants often described feeling like the generalists of the music business. Many of them also discussed the challenges the unbounded nature of their work posed.

The clauses in management agreements that outline the scope of the manager's functions and obligations belie the complexity of the role and its ever-expanding nature. Now that major recording labels have less power and control over new artists than they used to, power is shifting to emerging artists who derive leverage from their direct connections with their audiences—and this is impacting managers. The type of management agreements discussed in the survey typically state that the manager agrees to use all reasonable endeavours to seek and procure engagements for the artist in the 'entertainment industry'. The word 'entertainment' is often used rather than 'music' so as to broaden the scope.

In a typical management agreement, the manager agrees to use all reasonable endeavours to develop, promote and advance the artist's creative career. Further, the manager agrees to keep the artist abreast of all substantial negotiations they are conducting with third parties on their behalf. Usually, the scope of the role is limited by the inclusion of a clause stating that the manager is not obliged to provide the artist advice on personal taxation, investment or financial matters. There is usually no mention of how boundaries will be maintained in the relationship in the case that the artist suffers from mental ill health. The manager is exclusively authorised and empowered to engage and direct other people, firms or companies on the artist's behalf and in their name subject to any specific artist approval requirements that are also described in the agreement.

DOI: 10.4324/9781003388005-5

Music artist managers are generalists. Along with the artist, they get 'to see and touch all the jigsaw puzzle pieces that fit together to create the artist's career' (Frascogna & Hetherington, 2011, p. 6). These jigsaw puzzle pieces include the five main revenue streams: 'live performance, merchandise, song publishing, records, and sponsorship deals' (Morrow, 2006, p. 93). Becoming a manager helps create a broad understanding of the many facets of the music business ecosystem.

As discussed earlier, many managers described their role as the CEO of the artist's business, a role that involves strategising across this diverse array of revenue streams. However, on average, the 77 managers who participated in the survey each had five clients. The typical manager is thus simultaneously the CEO equivalent of five different businesses. Of these different artists' businesses, those that have leverage derived from existing connections with an audience or who are simply exceptionally talented often become more powerful within the music business, and harnessing this requires more time, effort and skill from their manager/CEO. These artists make more money and thus pay more through to their managers than their lower-leverage peers in the manager's stable. They demand more effort but also provide greater financial returns. This contrasts with earlier phases of the music business when major record labels held most of the power; artists and managers would agree one-sided recording agreements that were unlikely to recoup initial outlays in the hope they would make money from

> tickets and t-shirts. . . . We use records to try to create other income streams . . . we try and get the record company to spend as much as they can in order to lift the profile of the band as much as possible so that we have bigger ticket sales and bigger T-shirt sales and so there are more opportunities for sync rights.
>
> (Australian artist manager Gregg Donavan,
> as cited in Morrow, 2006, p. 139)

From the perspective of many of the research participants, in contrast to previous eras, the manager's role is ever expanding partly because recordings can now provide an income stream for them and the artists they manage if they can harness their newfound market power effectively. The changing power relations in the business make the manager's role more amorphous and all-encompassing than ever before.

Changing power relations

Power structures within the music business have changed, and this has influenced the remuneration structures and systems within it. To explain what is meant by the word 'power', Fleming and Spicer (2007) argued that there are two broad traditions. There is the normative tradition, which attempts to answer the utopian question: how should power relations be organised in society? The second tradition, inspired by the work of Niccolo Machiavelli (1515/1997), addresses the questions: 'How does power actually operate? How do people gain and maintain power within the realpolitik of social relations?' (Fleming & Spicer, 2007, p. 12). According to Fleming and Spicer (2007), twentieth-century social scientists involved in the latter tradition identified the following four 'faces' of power:

> The first face of power is coercion and involves one individual getting another to follow his/her orders. The second face involves the manipulation of agendas through 'behind the scenes' politicking. The third face of power is domination over the preferences and opinions of participants. The fourth face entails subjectification, whereby actors are constituted as subjects with certain understandings of themselves and the world around them.
>
> (p. 13)

In his well-researched book on the evolution of US-based major and independent record labels from the days of Tin Pan Alley through to 1990, Dannen (1991) chronicled the coercive power used by the pioneers of the record business. While he only wrote about the music business in the US, American cultural imperialism and the reach of multinational record companies makes his work relevant to the Australian context as well. Dannen critiqued many recording industry players from the early days, who were characterised as luminaries despite their links with organised criminals. Payola—for example, bribing a radio station employee to play a certain record over another in an attempt to ensure it became a hit—was rife. In the 1950s, gatekeepers were bribed with brown paper bags full of cash or threatened with baseball bats, while in the 1960s and 1970s, cash was used in addition to marijuana and LSD. Dannen noted that

> the pioneers deserve praise for their foresight but little for their integrity. Many of them were crooks. Their victims were usually poor blacks, the inventors of rock and roll, though whites did not fare much better. . . . Special mention is due to Herman Lubinsky, owner of Savoy Records in Newark, who recorded a star lineup of jazz, gospel, and rhythm and blues artists and paid scarcely a dime in royalties.
>
> (1991, p. 31)

The character Herman 'Hesh' Rabkin in the HBO television series *The Sopranos*, played by Jerry Adler, is a composite character based on the music mogul

Morris 'Mo' Levy. Dannen described how Levy founded Roulette Records in 1956 and alleged that he had a lifelong association with the Mafia:

> A Sephardic Jew . . . from the poorest section of the Bronx, Morris was never a member, but he did business with several crime families. The Genovese Family of New York cast the longest shadow over his career. . . . The record business has never shrunk from the Mob. By the end of World War II, the industry's best customers were jukebox operators, and many of them were mafiosi. Since the Depression, the Mafia has played a key role in artist management and booking (especially of black performers), pressing, and independent distribution.
>
> (1991, pp. 33–34)

Dannen (1991) also noted that rock historians tend to romanticise these pioneers, and in my earlier work I found that some music artist managers do too. I interviewed an influential Canadian music executive and music artist manager in 2010 who argued that

> to some degree, what's happening is we're beating the colour out of the whole thing. So to some degree everything's getting less interesting. . . . I like those old characters from the '50s and '60s who probably did everything wrong but ended up creating a world where some of the best music ever done was done, and people still love that music.
>
> (Morrow, 2018, p. 80)

This romanticisation of power relations between record labels, managers and the mafia in the 1950s and 1960s is odd given that record labels often abused their power to exploit the artists.

Record labels have used coercive power by making decisions on which music could become a hit. They directly attempted to force this upon consumers through the manipulation of broadcast media outlets though '"behind the scenes" politicking' (Fleming & Spicer, 2007, p. 13) by way of payola and other means. While radio DJs may have been bribed in the interests of artists and their managers, who may have been complicit in this behaviour in a competitive industry, the coercive power that record labels had was also turned against artists.

As introduced earlier, for Fleming and Spicer (2007), 'the third face of power is domination over the preferences and opinions of participants' (p. 13), and Giblin and Doctorow (2022) argued that, following the historical period Dannen (1991) discussed, major label record deals remained one-sided. They cited the case of the artist Prince in the early 1990s changing his name to an unpronounceable symbol in protest at the fact that he did not own his own master copyright in his recordings due to the recording agreement he signed in 1977 when he was 18 years old. They noted that

> this bitter fight was playing out at a time that major record labels had a vice grip on the industry. They controlled radio airplay, print and television media, as well as distribution into stores. And they were abusing that power in breathtaking ways.
>
> (Giblin & Doctorow, 2022, p. 52)

Giblin and Doctorow (2022) worked through several examples of low royalties in recording agreements and argued that the way the royalty stream is used to recoup advances paid by labels for recording costs was, and is, unfair. They noted that if artists did recoup their advance from their income— somewhere between 2 per cent and 12 per cent (2022, pp. 55–59) of net earnings from record sales—the label still owned the master copyright in their recordings. Giblin and Doctorow cited American guitarist Nile Rodgers to highlight this issue: 'The music business is the only business where after you pay off the mortgage on the house, they still own the house' (Rogers, as cited in Giblin & Doctorow, 2022, p. 54). While some artists can leverage licence deals instead of assigning their copyright to labels nowadays, Giblin and Doctorow continued: 'With few exceptions . . . contracts signed from the 1970s to the 2000s, when major labels were at their peak power and abuses against artists were most rife, still govern use of that music today' (2022, p. 57).

Indeed, when some record labels professed support for the Black Lives Matter movement in mid-2020, Josh Kun called out the hypocrisy by suggesting they 'start with amending contracts, distributing royalties, diversifying board rooms, and retroactively paying back all the black artists, and their families, they have built their empires on' (Kun, as cited in Giblin & Doctorow, 2022, p. 59). Influential independent label Beggars Group began forgiving heritage artists' recoupment debt after 15 years, and Sony announced in 2021 that they would do something similar (Giblin & Doctorow, 2022). Universal Music Group and Warner followed suit in 2022 (Brandle, 2022). CEO of Beggars Group Martin Mills also called for a minimum royalty rate of 15 per cent in 2016 (Ingham, 2016, 2020; Giblin & Doctorow, 2022, p. 59). In their influential research on music creators' earnings in the digital era for the UK's Intellectual Property Office, Hesmondhalgh et al. (2021) noted:

> The accounting information we received from an independent record company suggests that in some instances, at least, this model can work. This company has revised its legacy contracts so that all artists receive a minimum royalty rate of 25%. Recoupment is waived 15 years after a recording is released.
>
> (p. 122)

The one-sided record deals of the past are being undone in these ways, and new artists can negotiate higher royalties now too. Giblin and Doctorow (2022) posited that in the past, American R&B act TLC received 2 per cent of the USD 175 million generated by their music; in the 1950s and 1970s a 4 per cent royalty was common; during the CD boom in the late 1990s/early 2000s the average royalty was 7 per cent; while Radiohead's deal signed in 1991 featured a 12 per cent royalty (pp. 55–59). Nowadays, because recorded music is cheaper to produce and distribute and the internet has led to more competition, 'twenty-five percent is becoming standard. Some labels will pay 50 percent, especially if they don't pay an advance' (p. 58). Artists can now have a more equal relationship with labels, partnering with them to access capital, marketing support and distribution.

As one of the music lawyers I interviewed and cited in Chapter 3 noted the environment has changed and artists have more options now; they can sign directly to a label, either licensing or assigning the master copyright in their recordings; they can put their recordings out themselves; or they can release their music by way of a label services deal, which lies somewhere in between. Label services deals simply involve the artist using some of the services a label provides, but not 'full service'. The example given was a music distribution company advancing an artist $100,000 for marketing costs in exchange for the distributor receiving a 30 per cent participation in the income for three to four years with the artist receiving the balance, after which time the artist then receives 100 per cent if the advance is recouped.

However, while power relations within the music business have changed, and this has influenced the remuneration structures and systems, with both heritage and new artists in many instances being able to obtain better deals, major labels are still powerful, just in a different way. As Hesmondhalgh et al. (2021) noted: 'The industry has worked on a model whereby the risks involved in investing in new releases are compensated for by the returns of successful back catalogue recordings' (p. 122). Music streaming has made major labels' vast back catalogues of master copyrights—which in many instances they still own—more profitable due to the ease of access facilitated by streaming. Yet despite them now waiving some recoupment debts, the royalties they pay out are still determined by the deals of the past. Further, when it comes to new artists, the streaming system that the major labels had a central role in designing is essentially winner takes all, disproportionately benefiting the most successful international artists and the most powerful multinational major record labels (Giblin & Doctorow, 2022, p. 79). It is no surprise that a 2021 UK parliamentary enquiry found that

> aggregate information from the accounts of the major music companies show that, in the last six years, the major music companies are performing exceptionally well in terms of profit, and are continuing to grow. Between 2015 and 2019, disclosed major label turnover increased by 21 percent, but

operating profit grew by an unprecedented 64 percent and their operating profit margin on turnover increased from 8.7 percent to 11.8 percent. . . . Sony Music CEO Rob Stringer recently told shareholders that streaming has underpinned historic profit margins for the company.

(Digital, Culture, Media and Sport Committee,
House of Commons, 2021, p. 61)

Therefore the major record labels are still very dominant and very powerful; the bigger picture here is that they derive value from commercialising their back catalogues while streamlining their services when it comes to new signings by externalising the risks onto artists for funding new recordings, and the labour required to produce and promote these recordings onto managers, all the while generating a lot of revenue from their deep catalogues and the small number of successful new international artists who dominate streaming.

Managers' mental health

Alongside emerging artists' newfound power come newfound risks. A truism of the record business is that 'only one in ten signings make money' (McMartin & Eliezer, 2002, p. 9). Similarly, 'you have a better statistical chance of being struck by lightning than of having a number-one hit record or a top ten grossing concert tour' (Frascogna & Hetherington, 2011, p. 4). Although major record companies in the past were able to recover from a success rate of less than 10 per cent because of the overwhelming success of a minority of their artists (Frith, 2001, p. 35), the rise of label services deals, and the circular career development model discussed in Chapter 3 generally, means that much of the risk of product development is externalised onto artists themselves—or other investors—and this, alongside the fact that it does not cost as much to record nowadays, means that major record labels are not exposed to as much risk through product development costs as they were in the past. Some of the nine out of ten who lose money are losing the artist's money, not the label's, and managers who risk a lot of their time in attempting to develop projects lose out as well.

This externalisation of financial risk and workload has expanded the role of the music artist manager, and the pressure and stress of this expansion is impacting the mental health of some managers. Further, such pressure was exacerbated by the stresses of the COVID-19 pandemic and the shutdown of the live music business this involved, a topic that permeated the interviews given they were conducted in 2022–23. One manager I interviewed stated:

A lot of managers at the moment are burnt out or on the verge of burnout. 100 per cent. I mean, the best evidence of that is the last 48 hours of my life, telling everyone that I'm leaving as a result of burnout and mental health struggles and the reactions of everyone; I had two managers cry on my shoulder last night. That's evidence of the fact that, not just those two instances, but all of the conversations that I've had, in which managers are essentially telling me that they're on the verge themselves. Yeah, everyone's finding it hard. . . . I would say the principal reasons for burnout are just the incredible workload that is inherent in management.

(Interview 2)

This manager, who was leaving the business entirely despite having achieved remarkable commercial success, elaborated on the workload issue. They pointed out that one common reason for manager burnout is

the desire of so many artists in the modern context to stay independent. And that has come about for a variety of reasons. It always existed, but it's particularly relevant in the current context. The impact that that has on managers, of course, is the necessity for them to pick up the slack and essentially operate a record label at the same time. It's a management company that's rolling out tracks, and that's really significant. Often, they're not getting any extra compensation for that, it's just another extra part of the workload for a lot of artists when you don't have a record label.

(Interview 2)

Another manager who had recently stopped managing artists elaborated on this point:

The manager has to take on label services or label management anyway, to work with the distributors and get all the marketing sorted, and they're still just a manager. Oftentimes, they're investing their time and their money, with no access to the master, no actual fee, for doing that work of label management, it's just all absorbed into the 20 per cent, that once upon a time didn't include all of that work.

(Interview 5)

Obviously if an artist can connect with an audience independently, or via a distribution agreement like the one outlined in Chapter 3 and recounted earlier—whereby they earn a 70 per cent royalty for three to four years and thereafter 100 per cent once the AUD 100,000 advance is recouped—then the manager's commission on this income through the type of agreement outlined in Chapter 1 could be significant. However, without a relatively long post-term commission period in their agreement, they are carrying a lot of weight while sprinting across very insecure ground. The heart-palpitating stress this causes managers was articulated by the following participant:

It's just an incredible amount of stress. I think the fact that the only real way to have success and to approach a career now is to do it globally means that inevitably you're operating on a 24-hour time zone, and I think it's pretty tough to stay in good shape, mentally, operating that way. It's verging on unrealistic. It's not always as heavy going, as it is during album campaigns and certain tours. But if you're getting opportunities, what happens when things start going well, and there's not many resources—you might not have staff—you're touring internationally, everything's hard in every way, and you're like wearing that, and you're operating all around the clock and that's a structure that guarantees either, like, burnout or, like, a major breakdown, and it often makes it very hard to then get the benefit of what you've achieved up to that point; you're losing that because you can't mentally handle it.

(Interview 8)

The global nature of the contemporary music business clearly stretches managers' mental and physical capacities. Further anxiety is added by the threat that the client will be poached by another manager or international management firm:

It's quite fraught in the sense that you can do really well, you can pick the right artist, you create the opportunities and you can have everything going in the direction you want it to, and it seems almost inevitable that either the artist will want to quit, or they will fire you, or that the stress of running the operation will impact your own mental health, or personal life to the point that you also need to step away. The artist may see an international manager being a better option. You learn to deal with it better as you gain more experience, but I was fortunate to get through those times where it got really tough, both on a personal and a business level, and the number of challenging experiences managers in the community have means that many do not stay in management, and many leave the industry entirely.

(Interview 8)

I interviewed David Vodicka, who is one of Australian preeminent music lawyers, and he agreed that the role of an Australian music artist manager has expanded because of the transition to a global industry, but added that this transition has occurred without major music companies investing to assist Australian artists to connect with international audiences:

I think that there's a fundamental problem in the music industry across a number of sectors, not just management. What seems to have been missed in the transition to a global industry is that there needs to be adjustments at all levels. . . . A&R . . . there hasn't been investment, I think, by these big companies. So, they're surprised that the lack of success, or the lack of ability to transfer Australian artists into an international level also is part of this problem, because managers inevitably manage Australian acts, who then want to be successful internationally. If I look at our business, we very much transferred on our music practice to being an international practice where we deal with people internationally all the time, because that's basically the business. . . . You need an international game plan. . . . The skill shortage at management is reflected in labels and publishers.

(Interview 16)

Vodicka's overview of the Australian music business is useful for putting the stresses that the managers cited earlier articulated into a broader context. The perceived exodus of talented managers from the field that is causing a brain drain is accompanied by skills shortages within the ranks of major labels and song publishers, according to him. This is exacerbating the problem and causing a vicious spiral.

Artists' mental health

As was discussed in Chapter 3, the innate stress of the music artist manager's role is partly due to half the role being outward looking towards the music business, and half being inward looking towards the artist. As outlined earlier, the outward-looking side of the role has in many cases expanded—though the inward-looking side of the role has expanded too, for example, managers helped manage music artists' mental health during the COVID-19 pandemic.

Musgrave (2022) examined media representations of musicians' mental health during the first year of the COVID-19 pandemic in the United Kingdom. He found that two dominant narratives emerged. The first narrative concerned the employment anxiety stemming from the loss of income, and the second concerned the existential anxiety faced by many musicians caused by a loss of purpose. Musgrave cited evidence suggesting that, compared to other occupational groups, musicians experience higher levels of mental ill health 'and may even have lower life expectancy' (p. 12). He cited a range of factors that are acknowledged in the literature as causing emotional distress. The factors causing emotional distress stem from the psychosocial working conditions of musicians and include

financial precarity . . . performance anxiety . . . anti-social working hours . . . the prevalence of alcohol or substance use . . . high levels of pressure to succeed . . . the negative impact of musical work on family life . . . missing loved ones whilst touring . . . and the particular challenges and stressors faced by female musicians.

(p. 13)

Add to this regular adrenaline crashes post-performance, long-term separations from not only family but community, as well as poor food and sleep (Giblin & Doctorow, 2022, p. 97). The evidence Musgrave cited suggested that these emotional stresses were exacerbated by the outbreak of the COVID-19 pandemic and its associated lockdowns. In addition to these challenges, there was a tendency for the research participants to link artistic creativity with mental ill health. For example, Australian artist manager John Watson noted that

> people with mental health challenges over-index in the creative space. There's a chicken-and-egg element to that, but it's widely accepted. . . . The manager is joined at the hip with those people and in any sphere of life, when you are joined at the hip with someone who is going through mental health battles, that can take quite a toll on the person. Psych' students would talk a lot about responsible boundaries for how to help a client without getting too enlisted in their problems. Managers, by default, inherit those issues, and their business is at stake . . . there's an inherent instability, not in every relationship, maybe not even in most relationships, but in a significant number of relationships that arise out of the fact that there is a certain over-indexing of unstable people who have a genius gift for creating beautiful things.
>
> (Interview 13)

However, in contrast to this perspective, one that was commonly shared by the research participants, leading social psychologist and creativity researcher Keith Sawyer (2012) noted that

> the connections between creativity, schizophrenia, and manic-depressive illness are intriguing, but when you review all of the scientific research, the bottom line is that there isn't convincing evidence of a connection between mental illness and creativity. . . . The consensus of all major creativity researchers today is that there's no link between mental illness and creativity.
>
> (p. 171)

Although the tendency to believe in a connection between creativity and mental illness was common in the research data, there is a need to be critical here. Nevertheless, though, when these comments are considered within the context of Musgrave's (2022) research (see also Gross & Musgrave, 2020), it is evident that artists' lives are not easy, and the boundaryless nature of the music artist manager's role means that the inward-looking side of it often expands in scope. Watson continued:

> A lot of managers are drawn to it by the need to help those people. I certainly know that at times, I had been. The thing that really kept me coming

back for more in difficult situations was I felt personally, emotionally, obligated to try to help a person that I could see struggling. And so, I think that there's that dynamic to the health of managers too. Because, where do you put all of that, at the end of the day, when that person's confessed their deepest, darkest to you and your spouse is sick of hearing you talk about it, or whatever, and you can't go tell the person at the record company because they're not going to invest any money if they realise just how fragile this whole operation is. So, it can be a very solitary job.

(Interview 13)

The inward-looking, solitary side of the role, therefore, has expanded in many cases because the stresses artists are under have increased in recent years, and the boundaries between the manager's role and the role that mental health professionals could and should play are porous. This in turn can undermine the manager's mental health due to the isolated way in which they work. Another Australian music artist manager who participated, Leigh Treweek, noted that

most managers are sole traders. They're dealing with a lot. And there is no one to turn to. The AAM obviously creates a community which is incredibly important to what we do, and I think a lot of managers would be lost without it, but it is a lonely job.

(Interview 7)

The role is therefore ill-defined in terms of emotional labour and boundaries.

An ill-defined role

Senior Australian music lawyer David Vodicka noted that the role of the music artist manager is also ill-defined in terms of geographical scope:

I think the tricky bit for me is the middle ground and the big problem is that, as the industry has transitioned from a domestic market to a global market, the areas where managers could make a more sustainable living in the past have gone. Where you had a sort of ring-fenced geo-blocked market, you had more ability to have local successes.

(Interview 16)

The role is ill-defined in terms of how managers can go about it: 'How do you break new acts? It's like the majors don't even know how to do that now . . . pop hits are broken, either totally by or significantly by TikTok' (Focus Group 2); and the artist often has an ill-defined understanding of the manager's role: 'I do think there's a little bit of an understanding gap here, between what artists understand the job to be and what it actually is for their manager' (Dawson et al., 2022). Though, unfortunately, amidst all this ill defi-nition, what is increasingly being clearly defined is the time span of the artist's career: it is often short, as artist manager John Watson noted: 'The successes that are happening are track-based rather than artist-based . . . we are moving back to shorter careers, typically, for artists' (Interview 13).

In addition to these stresses and pressures that managers are under in the current era, there are cultural differences in the way in which the Australian live music market operates. This too places more weight on the manager: they and the artist often self-promote club tours. This contrasts with other territo-ries, such as the US and UK, where there are often local promoters in each city who will take the risk on promoting club shows. Australian artist manager Jess Keeley discussed this point:

> I don't know why this happened. But promoters in this country don't do small tours, club tours. And that means that the artist self-promotes the whole time. So, the artist has an agent who would book the tour and then the artist and manager are responsible for advertising and marketing that tour and working out the routing and doing all of the heavy lifting. I cannot believe that that is the setup in Australia.
>
> (Interview 4)

This is a situation I have previously argued (Morrow, 2013) is due to the legacy in Australia of the management company Dirty Pool effectively cut-ting out promoters and agents in the late 1970s. Instead of using promoters and agents, they did the work themselves as managers along with their artists. They did this to address the extensive graft and corruption within the live music business in Australia at the time. Touring Australia is not easy due to the relatively small population being spread out across a vast land mass. Hav-ing artists and managers take the risk on promoting, and then either incurring a loss or reaping a return from live music at the entry to mid-level of the Aus-tralian live music industry, can also exacerbate the problems outlined earlier in this chapter.

Conclusion

Unsustainable workloads that lead to managers burning out have the by-product of muting resistance to monopolistic label power, to the detri-ment of artists. Major labels have essentially admitted that the past deals they did with artists were unfair through the way in which they are subsequently tweaking them. When knowledgeable, experienced and talented managers leave the business, artists are less able to resist major label dominance and power, and nowadays streaming service dominance and power, and in the live music industry—as will be discussed in the next chapter—live music promoters such as Live Nation's dominance and power. While in the recorded music industry, new artists can now often leverage more favourable terms, the by-product of these better deals can be manager burnout; when artists remain independent or do label services deals, the risk and reward that used to rest with record labels and song publishers is externalised onto them and their management. While some managers react to having to do the work of the record label and song publisher as well as being the manager by becoming labels and publishers themselves, as I argue in the next chapter, this introduces conflicts of interest: when managers become both the label and the manager, they negotiate with themselves. There may be better ways of addressing the problems stemming from the seemingly ever-expanding role of music artist managers outlined in this chapter—both in terms of the outward-looking aspects and the inward-looking ones—through new models for music artist manager retention. This is what the next chapter explores.

References

Brandle, L. (2022, April 1). Universal music group is waiving unrecouped debts for heritage acts. *The Music Network*. https://themusicnetwork.com/universal-waving-unrecouped-debts/

Dannen, F. (1991). *Hit men: Power brokers and fast money inside the music business*. Knopf Doubleday Publishing Group.

Dawson, O., Keeley, J., & Carey, G. (2022, September 7). *Sustainable relationships? The value of management partnerships* [Panel presentation, G. Morrow, Chair]. BigSound, Brisbane, Queensland.

Digital, Culture, Media and Sport Committee, House of Commons. (2021). *Economics of music streaming*. https://publications.parliament.uk/pa/cm5802/cmselect/cmcumeds/50/5007.htm

Fleming, P., & Spicer, A. (2007). *Contesting the corporation: Struggle, power and resistance in organizations*. Cambridge University Press. https://doi.org/10.1017/CBO9780511628047

Frascogna, X. M., & Hetherington, H. L. (2011). *This business of artist management: The standard reference to all phases of managing a musician's career from both the artist's and manager's point of view*. Crown.

Frith, S. (2001). The popular music industry. In J. Street, S. Frith, & W. Straw (Eds.), *The Cambridge companion to pop and rock* (pp. 26–52). Cambridge University Press. https://doi.org/10.1017/CCOL9780521553698.004

Giblin, R., & Doctorow, C. (2022). *Chokepoint capitalism: How big tech and big content captured creative labor markets and how we'll win them back*. Scribe Publications.

Gross, S. A., & Musgrave, G. (2020). *Can music make you sick? Measuring the price of musical ambition*. University of Westminster Press. https://doi.org/10.2307/j.ctv199tddg

Hesmondhalgh, D., Osborne, R., Sun, H., & Barr, K. (2021). *Music creators' earnings in the digital era*. Intellectual Property Office. https://assets.

publishing.service.gov.uk/government/uploads/system/uploads/attachment_data/file/1020133/music-creators-earnings-report.pdf

Ingham, T. (2016, February 15). Martin Mills: Majors must pay artists fairly if we're to win safe harbour fight. *Music Business Worldwide*. www.music-businessworldwide.com/martin-mills-majors-must-pay-artists-fairly-if-were-to-beat-youtube/

Ingham, T. (2020, June 8). Labels could start helping Black artists by adjusting old record deals. *Rolling Stone*. www.rollingstone.com/pro/features/music-black-artists-old-record-deals-1011447/

Machiavelli, N. (1997). *The prince*. Penguin. (Original work published 1515)

McMartin, M., & Eliezer, C. (2002). *The music manager's manual* (Eds. M. McMartin, C. Eliezer, & B. Brown). Music Manager's Forum (Australia).

Morrow, G. (2006). *Managerial creativity: A study of artist management practices in the Australian popular music industry* [Doctoral thesis, Macquarie University]. Figshare. https://figshare.mq.edu.au/articles/thesis/Managerial_creativity_a_study_of_artist_management_practices_in_the_Australian_popular_music_industry/19427489

Morrow, G. (2013). The influence of dirty pool on the Australian live music industry: A case study of boy & bear. In P. Tschmuck, P. L. Pearce, & S. Campbell (Eds.), *Music business and the experience economy: The Australasian case* (pp. 135–152). Springer. https://doi.org/10.1007/978-3-642-27898-3_9

Morrow, G. (2018). *Artist management: Agility in the creative and cultural industries*. Routledge.

Musgrave, G. (2022). 'Losing work, losing purpose': Representations of musicians' mental health in the time of COVID-19. In G. Morrow, D. Nordgård, & P. Tschmuck (Eds.), *Rethinking the music business: Music contexts, rights, data, and COVID-19* (pp. 11–28). Springer International Publishing. https://doi.org/10.1007/978-3-031-09532-0_2

Sawyer, R. K. (2012). *Explaining creativity: The science of human innovation* (2nd ed.). Oxford University Press.

5   New models for music
artist manager retention

Introduction

The music artist manager's role is to advocate for music artists. This often involves negotiating for them to licence the master copyrights in their recordings to other entities only for a set term, rather than in perpetuity; helping artists to directly manage their relationship with their audience via social media; helping artists remain independent for as long as possible to better their position in subsequent negotiations with record labels and song publishers; or helping them do label services deals, or remain independent entirely, instead of directly signing to major or independent labels in long-term plays for sustainability. While these efforts can better position artists, enabling them to achieve their long-term career goals, as I outlined in Chapter 4, they also increase the manager's workload. Further, while better deals for individual artists can help, the main reason why music artists earn so little from the cultural products they create is that, as Giblin and Doctorow (2022) noted, 'the most profitable supply chains have been colonized by powerful corporations who use their control over chokepoints to co-opt most of its value' (p. 142). The AAM is a unique collective of managers who can work together to mitigate this co-option for the betterment of music artists. However, for music artist managers to be able to more effectively advocate for artists both individually in the ways outlined earlier, and collectively through the AAM, new models for music artist manager retention are needed.

In this chapter, the new models for music artist manager retention that are presented are not designed to simply enable managers to muscle their way in between music artists and their audiences to capture a greater share of the monetary value that flows between them. The value managers bring to their relationship with artists is the ability to increase the size of the artist's piece of the pie. While the models and solutions presented in this chapter will increase the manager's share, theoretically, by growing their slice, the artist's slice too will grow. A healthy, strong and independent music artist manager community—one that can offer frank and fearless advice to clients—is needed for artists to be able to wrestle back some of the value that is co-opted by

DOI: 10.4324/9781003388005-6

powerful corporations. This is a David-versus-Goliath scenario, and music artists' livelihoods are at stake too.

As was outlined in Chapter 3, rather than reinforcing the perception of some managers that there are broad norms and standards when it comes to their business model, the lawyers who participated highlighted that there are many different types of agreements being used in the field. That there is diversity in these agreements suggests a need for some managers to set aside the illusion of permanence of industry standards, and to instead argue for best fit in terms of strategy, goals and the value proposition managers bring to negotiations. The ideas set forth in this chapter come from the research interviews conducted for this book as well as the music press, and they represent the beginning of a conversation, not the end. The best solutions for each individual manager and artist are likely to be unique to them. Therefore, please read this chapter critically and build on the ideas contained within it—or come up with new ones. Doing so will hopefully lead to the establishment of a more sustainable music ecosystem.

Increasing financial rewards for managers

In 2019, Luke Girgis (2019) published an opinion piece in which he argued that, because record labels and song publishers are spread so thinly nowadays in terms of artist-to-staff ratios, artist managers arguably have the most influence on any individual artists' career development, often developing their careers and brands from scratch. Because, as was also outlined in my previous chapters, they are paid the same, or less, than they were when labels and publishers had higher artist-to-staff ratios. According to Girgis, managers either leave the music business, move sideways to more secure roles in the business, or start record labels, publishing companies or touring companies in addition to their management role in order to diversify their income, to obtain an equity stake in what they are building and to develop exit strategies. Girgis argued that the current system disincentivises managers from concentrating solely on management.

When considering how other industries retain their leaders, Girgis (2019) noted that 'most tech companies offer stock options (real equity). . . . Why are artists not treating their managers, i.e. their CEOs, the same way?' The solution Girgis put forth was for managers to be given master points (a royalty) for each recording the artist they manage releases and a 'small publishing share' in the artist's songs. This would give 'the artist manager . . . real equity in the business they are building'. The precedent for the type of agreement that this would involve are the record producer agreements that were outlined in Chapter 3. While record producers get points because they were in the studio with the artist investing time and ideas into the recording process, and managers usually are not contributing in this way during the artistically creative process, the argument here is that the CEO of a supermarket chain may be given stock options whilst not contributing labour on the farm that produced the goods sold. While some of the managers interviewed did not agree with this argument that managers should also get points, others thought that the privileging of artistic creativity over managerial creativity (Morrow, 2006) by giving points to record producers and not managers was problematic. Managers are often executive producers of recordings, and, if they were given points, managers could generate assets that could earn them passive, capital income in addition to their commissions, thus providing a more viable business model and assisting them in retirement. Girgis claimed that when he discussed this model with managers, he was often met with awkward responses. There was a perception that this model did not put artists first. Girgis argued counter to this perception, stating that it did put artists first because this model would help artists' managers focus on them, rather than splitting their attention because they have also set up a record label, etc.

Further, managers *do* often obtain equity in the businesses they are building by setting up record labels and becoming song publishers. While the difference between management companies and record labels is that the latter usually invest capital into projects, while management companies traditionally only invest time. One Australian artist manager interviewed noted that all managers have to do to mitigate the entire discussion in Chapter 3 of whether there are industry standard terms for managers is change the word 'manager' to 'label':

> When you're a manager and you're charging 20 per cent, you're doing all this work. And you pivot to another area where, essentially, the same thing is happening, you're doing work, or you're offering money or time, and you get more things . . . but because you called yourself a label, rather than a manager, everyone's like, 'Oh, that's correct. Yes, that's standard.' It's just simply a change of word.
>
> (Interview 5)

However, when managers do simply change the word 'manager' to 'label' and/or 'publisher', they introduce conflicts of interest and the problematic opportunity to double dip into the artist's revenue streams. Double dipping in this scenario would involve the artist manager receiving income as the record label or song publisher while also commissioning the artist's share of the recording or song publishing income as the artist manager (see Morrow, 2018, pp. 93–97). Further, by becoming the label, they can also get in the way of deal making with larger entities that could help grow the artist's career, thus potentially undermining their ability to advocate for the artist. This is a topic I covered in my earlier work (see Morrow, 2018, pp. 36–37), and while there are solutions to these issues, which I will not repeat here, they are complicated. From my perspective, what Girgis (2019) proposed is a neater solution for rewarding and incentivising managers, and I agree that it would help them to focus on management. The one caveat to this, though, is that, according to some of the research participants, there is a risk that some managers would be over-rewarded by the model that Girgis proposed: 'There would be managers who would be hugely overpaid if a master share and a publishing share were put in place. There'd be managers who could not justify that, because they're bull bars' (Interview 13).

There is also the risk that artists could agree to share revenue in perpetuity in these ways but then have their relationship with the manager quickly collapse, meaning that they would be giving away too much relative to what they got in return. Yet, despite these risks, for Australian artist manager John Watson, the general principle of what Girgis proposed is sound:

> There would be managers who have not received that, who would have every reason to feel bitter over that fact. So, I think it's a case-by-case situation, but I definitely think there are many cases where some kind of ongoing share of revenue—whether that's on the master side, the publishing side, whether it's by commission, or whatever mechanism the parties agree. If it is accepted that the publisher and the record company and the producer are growing the pie in a way that endures for perpetuity, why is it inconceivable that the manager is also growing the pie in a way that endures for perpetuity?
>
> (Interview 13)

Further, in a reiteration of arguments made in Chapter 3 about the value proposition a manager brings to their negotiation with the artist, senior Australian music lawyer David Vodicka pointed out:

> If you have 5% publishing on every track from the get-go and you're able to do that because the artist is young, inexperienced, whatever it is, they agreed to do that, because they believe that that's valid. And then if the management agreement doesn't last but the artist becomes very successful, you're likely going to have an artist who's fairly pissed off. If you're a manager at a certain level in this market, who has proven success, or is perceived to have shepherded artists to a certain level of success, I think it substantially increases your ability to argue the point. If you're an inexperienced manager, it's quite hard to sustain requests of that type.
>
> (Interview 16)

London-based Australian artist manager Rowan Brand made the point that a manager's points/royalties could be administered by way of direct payments from collecting societies:

> I also think if managers who can have these kinds of business models where they're either stakeholders in the business, as co-owners, or whether they have long-term interests on a songwriting on a publisher level or—and

this is real fantasy land—but if there was a way that the precedent whereby APRA [APRA AMCOS Australasian Performing Right Association and Australasian Mechanical Copyright Owners Society] allows producers to be cut in on a songwriting level could be replicated for managers. You can also do that with neighbouring rights; there's a structure for it and it's seen as something that's quite normal. If there was a way to normalise that conversation so that managers could also participate there as executive producers, or however that needs to be philosophised, and if there was a system by which that could be done, a framework where artists can go 'Do you have a manager? Do you want to cut them in? Tick a box here.' Something like that, then that might also help to normalise some of these procedures, and I think put more stability into the business.

(Interview 14)

If there is a precedent set for music producers to receive enduring entitlements directly from collecting societies upon receipt of a letter of direction from the artist, then perhaps this arrangement could work for managers as well.

Post-term commissions

Giving managers master points for each recording the music artist releases and a small publishing share in the artist's songs—by way of agreements that are like record producer agreements—is quite a dramatic departure from the type of management agreements outlined in Chapter 1. The general principle here is enduring entitlements, and there is already a clause in typical management agreements that can be adjusted to provide this: the post-term commission clause. A more palatable option for strategically incentivising managers to solely focus on management could simply be to extend the timeframe of the manager's post-term commission by having it scale down to a certain percentage in perpetuity. This could be negotiated instead of managers receiving points on masters.

This is not a new idea. When I was completing my PhD in 2006, veteran Australian/Canadian music artist manager Michael McMartin proposed to me that managers bring a certain talent to their role that should be rewarded in perpetuity, and this argument no doubt well and truly predates my discussion with him. An example of this type of post-term clause, sometimes called a 'post-termination' clause, would be for 100 per cent of the percentage set out in the management commission clause (for example 20 per cent) to be paid for the 12 months following the date of the termination of the agreement; then 75 per cent of the percentage set out in the management commission clause for the next 12-month period; then 50 per cent for the next 12 months; and then thereafter in perpetuity 25 per cent of the percentage set out in the management commission clause (so 5 per cent of the artist's revenue from records and song publishing if the starting management commission is

20 per cent). This contrasts with agreements that may have, say, a five-year span in total because, while the first three years may be the same as earlier, rather than having 25 per cent in perpetuity, this 25 per cent is just for the fourth and fifth years. Even this example of a clause with a five-year span is more favourable to managers than the three-year post-term commission structure that was frequently cited by the participants. For example, one Australian music artist manager noted: 'For the majority of my career, the idea of post-term commissions was really only three years, and it's really only applied to the recordings and the songs, not merchandise, not live, not other things' (Interview 5). Note that, in these examples, these provisions do not apply where the agreement is terminated by the manager or by the artist in response to the manager's breach of contract.

The question then becomes: to which of the artist's revenue streams does this post-term commission pertain? Typically, the artist agrees to pay the manager all sums outlined in the management commission clause for engagements and contracts entered during the term of the agreement, even if the sums have not been received at the time of termination of the agreement. Regarding revenue from sound recordings and song publishing, where the recordings are first released for sale to the public within three months after the date of termination of the agreement, the manager is entitled to receive a percentage from all income earned from them throughout the world after the date of termination of the agreement. Such post-term commissions are usually different to the idea outlined earlier of managers receiving points on the masters because, as will be outlined later, post-term commission structures usually taper off after a set period of time. In contrast, points on masters continue in perpetuity. A post-term commission in perpetuity is like having points on the masters.

These elements of the post-term clause translate to the manager getting the commission on the live performance engagements that were booked during the term of the agreement, even if the live performances are yet to take place and be remunerated. Other than this, the particular post-term commission clause outlined earlier does not involve the manager participating in the artist's live performance income in an enduring way. Managers do, however, have ongoing entitlements to shares in the revenue derived from the exploitation of the copyright in the recordings produced and music written during the term of the management agreement. In the research interviews, the participants presented various arguments concerning whether managers should receive post-term commissions from recording revenue, song publishing revenue, live performance income and merchandising income. There is also one music press article, Udell (2019), which is an op-ed response to the Girgis (2019) piece cited earlier, in which the author argued that post-termination participation in revenue should include new recordings that are produced after termination as well. I will now consider these arguments in turn.

As I outlined in Chapter 4, the economics of music streaming are such that major and independent record labels are today forgiving artists' recoupment debts after 15 years and some are revising royalties because the way in which their catalogues generate revenue on the 'back end' has changed (Giblin & Doctorow, 2022, p. 59; Ingham, 2020). This change is also grounds for managers to argue that enduring entitlements by way of post-term commissions in perpetuity are warranted. Old record deals have changed due to the economics of music streaming, and it is time that outdated management agreements change too. Streaming has changed the parameters for major and independent record labels, and they have been willing to revise their old deals. The new operating context makes their legacy recording agreements look even more one-sided than they originally did. Likewise, as senior Australian music lawyer David Vodicka stated (as quoted in Chapter 3), 'the way that revenue is now generated for artists, having a three-year post-term commission for the amount of time and effort you invest in an artist, to me, makes no sense as a business' (Interview 16).

Enduring entitlements for managers on the recordings and songs that were produced during their term by way of longer post-term commission structures thus make sense in the age of music streaming. Such claims present a neat solution to incentivise managers as they do not involve asking up front for a larger percentage of the artist's finite revenue. Rather, enduring entitlements are paid later and only become significant if the project is, or becomes, commercially successful. If an artist's strategic objectives include attempting to obtain a better share of recording and publishing revenue from the dominant multinational corporations in the music business, then retaining talented and independent managers by way of this mechanism makes sense: the manager's post-term commission would be a piece of their much larger pie.

When asked why he thought the percentage for the enduring post-term entitlement should be 25 per cent of the, for example, 20 per cent commission—so 5 per cent of the artist's revenue from recordings and song publishing would be invoiced—veteran Australian/Canadian music artist manager Michael McMartin posited:

> I think it should be there continually. But no more than say, 5 or 10 per cent, which then allows the artists to give a new manager a percentage of that income as an incentive to be out and exploiting it.
>
> (Interview 12)

McMartin further argued: 'If you're a member of the band, and you leave the band, you get your royalties in perpetuity, if you played on that album. And I don't see any difference between that and the manager' (Interview 12).

Explaining his rationale for the post-term commission clauses his management company puts in their agreements, London-based Australian artist manager Rowan Brand commented:

> We ensure that we have a long-term stake in the success of the projects that we work on with our artists. And that usually is reflected in the form of lengthy post-term commissions on recordings and publishing that we help to release and lift off the ground. Especially since the advent of streaming and the changes in the way that income is earned from recordings and publishing . . . if we don't put those contracts in place, then the risk is we put two years into running a campaign, we finish working with the artist after four or five years and at that point, even if it's a successful release, it still may not have recouped just yet. And so, there's a risk that we put all that work in, we do amazing work for the artists, and they are the 100 percent beneficiary of all of that. And we don't think that's fair.
>
> (Interview 14)

Despite this rationale, however, the role of music lawyers—which was discussed at length in Chapter 3—comes into play here. Brand noted:

> Those arguments are often long and difficult with artists' lawyers and we have walked away from multiple deals in the last couple of years with artists who we love and really would love to work with. But we've not been able to come to agreement on these kinds of philosophical ideas and we have to protect our business model.
>
> (Interview 14)

From the perspective of the research participants, it seems unfair for lawyers to advise managers that they cannot earn any post-term commissions after three years—which can mean that managers earn little from helping artists generate these revenue streams—when lawyers themselves provide an expensive service.

According to one Australian music artist manager, this problem is particularly pronounced when working with artists who are more critically acclaimed than commercially successful in the short term:

> I had a lot of success, critically, with a . . . band . . . and almost zero royalty income, very minimal. Very successful album. Unbelievably acclaimed, clearly one of the top ten most acclaimed records of the year. Hasn't recouped and won't that soon. Post-terms, now that I've just left it, are going to account for next to nothing on that record. If it does eventually earn some money, it might be long tail on streaming in five, 10 years, 15 years' time or potentially even better when the artist gets the rights back, on a well-structured deal, they can put it up with a service and get 97% of that streaming income. That can work well for the artists later in

their life. For the manager, they might not be around by then and so the lack of IP ownership and the fact that it's so long tail is an issue.

(Interview 8)

In response to the question of whether the scope of the post-term commission clause should include future live performance revenue, several participants noted that, for example, 'there are some managers I know who do take a post-term commission on live' (Interview 14). This is because live performance income is the main source of income for music artists (Tschmuck, 2017, p. 125) and because recoupment[1] means that record labels do not pay any royalties to artists until any advance that was paid and used by the artist to live and to produce recordings is recouped by the royalty amount.

This means that this revenue source can take a long time to become a stream to artists instead of trickling into their pool of recoupment debt; and it may never become one if their label does not forgive recoupment debt. As was discussed earlier, some major and independent record labels are forgiving recoupment debt after 15 years, and some are revising royalty amounts in old agreements (Giblin & Doctorow, 2022, p. 59; Ingham, 2020). This suggests that there are many established artists who have not recouped their advances and, given that royalties are only paid to them after doing so, have not received any royalties despite the music streaming boom for record labels. Regarding the percentage of live income in the mix, one research participant noted that 'the average successful business these days—this is my understanding from talking to the biggest accountants and bookkeepers in the music industry— generates about 65 percent of their income from live' (Interview 1). While these are arguments for including live performance income within the scope of post-term commission clauses, artist manager Rowan Brand provided the following rationale for his management company not including it in their agreements:

> If you think about a recording, the workflow goes from making, conceiving the recording, to putting the release plan in place, to putting the first single out, putting the record out, to working out the promo afterwards. That can be a two-year project, generally speaking, sometimes even longer. And any income earned from that really starts in earnest after the record is out. . . . So, the income profile of that project is even longer, say five to ten years. For touring, that's not the case. From booking the show, or procuring the show, papering [contracting] it, and then the show happening, it's very rarely 12 months. And the payment happens once the show is done, usually within a week of when the show is done. So, you've got a very neatly bookended project, with its own P&L [profit and loss statement], with no long ongoing income implications. And for that reason, philosophically, it doesn't sit as well with us . . . there's no long-term income to be chasing from the individual show.

(Interview 14)

When it comes to post-term commission clauses, while some of the participants were aware that it is the brand value that they helped to create during the term that enables artists to be booked onto prestigious festivals or sell out their tours after their tenure as manager, they were often also mindful of the need to leave room for later managers to be able to generate meaningful commissions and revenue.

Live income is important here given that the dominant corporations in the recorded music and song publishing industries siphon off much of the value created by artists through their recordings and songs. There are just three record labels that control almost 70 per cent of the global recorded music market (Giblin & Doctorow, 2022, p. 56). These labels, Universal Music Group, Sony Music Entertainment and Warner Music Group, also own the three song publishing companies that control almost 60 per cent of the global commercial song rights (Giblin & Doctorow, 2022). After a series of mergers and acquisitions, the world's three biggest music publishing companies are now Universal Music Publishing Group, Sony Music Publishing and Warner Chappell Music. This represents a massive aggregation of copyrights and means that if any individual artist and independent manager desire to work with a major label, they have to negotiate with a larger corporation than comparable artists and managers did in the past. This makes having a strong, independent and sustainable music artist management community even more important.

The major music business corporations need to be critically examined from an artist's perspective. For example, when record labels maximise 'breakage'—'a term that originally referred to a deduction for the costs of broken physical records, on which artists would not receive royalties' (Giblin & Doctorow, 2022, p. 71) but that now refers to any revenue that cannot be attributed to a specific use of songs or recordings—artists do not receive any revenue, and therefore this has a flow-on effect on managers and their management commissions and post-term commissions. The fact that some major record labels maximise charges to breakage in the age of music streaming was evidenced by the 2015 leak of a contract between Spotify and Sony Music Entertainment (see Giblin & Doctorow, 2022, p. 70) whereby Spotify paid Sony an advance of USD 5 million, though, if users did not stream enough of their music for this to be allocated to artists, Sony kept the balance as 'breakage'. Further, 'accounting errors' made by labels have historically been so endemic that it has been standard practice for years for managers of commercially successful artists to engage auditors to work through the label's books (Philips, 2002). For artists and managers alike, revenue from their recorded music and their songs often does not flow easily. There are, therefore, several reasons why the inclusion of live performance income in managers' post-term commission clauses was vigorously debated by the research participants.

While live performance income is important for artists and managers in the context of them being squeezed by the increasingly monopolistic multinational corporations who exert their market power in the recorded music and

song publishing industries, unfortunately a similar march towards monopoli-
sation is occurring at the top end of the live music industry as well. This has
implications for appropriate models for artist manager retention that go beyond
the question of whether future live performance income is included within the
scope of post-term commission clauses. One development concerning live performance income that the interviewees reported was that the US-based multinational entertainment company Live Nation is continuing to acquire music
artist management companies. As one Australian artist manager noted,

> I actually don't think it's artists that should be giving equity in their busi-
> ness. I feel now it might be more beneficial for the bigger corporations who
> own most of the music to be thinking about equity in management, and in
> management companies. So that would mean sustained support for man-
> agers in an agreement that serves the artists, so they have equity. That's
> because it's already happening; Live Nation own a bunch of management
> companies. That's them investing in the managers . . . what needs to shift
> now as far as the skills shortage goes is that the investment should be in
> the people [managers] not just in the artists. There's lots of management
> companies that have side agreements with different bigger corporates.
>
> (Interview 4)

While this model would help to address several of the problems outlined
in this book concerning the lack of support for managers, direct investment
in management companies by corporations such as Live Nation potentially
introduces conflicts of interest; it is somewhat of a Faustian bargain. In my
previous work (Morrow, 2018, pp. 110–111) one of the participants argued
that vertical integration with such corporations risks the manager becoming
a Judas goat[2]: 'To me [this] is almost sabotage. It's very dangerous' (p. 110).
While the instances being discussed in my previous work involved managers establishing joint ventures with major record labels, managers no longer
working independently of Live Nation is problematic for a similar reason:
by vertically integrating every element of live music production, there is a
risk that this corporation could sap artists' and independent managers' primary lifeblood: live performance income. Discussing the Australian situation,
Sainsbury (2022) noted that

> Live Nation, whose third-biggest shareholder is Saudi Arabia's Public
> Investment Fund . . . has over the past decade bought up more than a
> dozen Australian music festivals, ticketing companies, music agencies and
> venues, including Splendour in the Grass, Falls Festival, Spilt Milk, Tick-
> etmaster and Moshtix.

Sainsbury (2022) noted that industry insiders estimate that Live Nation along
with two other US-based touring companies, TEG and AEG, 'collectively

control at least 85 per cent of the Australian live music market'. This amount of power in the Australian live music market is unprecedented, and it dramatically reduces the ability of Australian music artist managers and live booking agents to negotiate reasonable terms for music artists when it comes to their live performances.

By merging with Ticketmaster in 2010, the world's largest ticketing company, and by purchasing major Australian ticketing company Moshtix in 2019 (Sainsbury, 2022), Live Nation has the potential to use its bird's-eye view of the live music business to be the ultimate poacher by using real-time ticketing data to swoop in and 'take over acts that have been developed by independent managers when they are just about to break through' (Giblin & Doctorow, 2022, p. 98).[3] While 'it is well known that if a manager is called a "trouble manager", the record company will try and remove him [sic] from the artists' (Morrow, 2018, p. 110), the fact that Live Nation can also potentially work to remove independent managers is not good for artists, or for the music business ecology overall. How can the manager negotiate the best terms for the artist with the live music promoter when the promoter owns the management company? If independent managers cannot obtain more favourable terms for their businesses, enabling them to become more sustainable by way of enduring entitlements and the like, and the only management companies that can survive are those that have been acquired by Live Nation, then this will supercharge Live Nation's attempts to monopolise the live music industry to the detriment of music artists.

Other ways to increase managers' share

Rather than playing into this centralisation of power in the music business, there are potentially new ways to decentralise power and ownership in the business. Joel Connolly, a former Australian music artist manager who now works for Australian venture capital company Blackbird, who was introduced towards the end of Chapter 3, wrote a follow-up piece to the article introduced earlier. In the earlier piece, Connolly (2021a) argued that there are built-in and systematic ways in which music artists are denied opportunities to build direct relationships with their customers. In the follow-up piece, entitled 'Decentralising the music industry: Ideas on equity financing, the creator economy, bitcoin', he argued that music artists have new opportunities to claim some of the power they have heretofore been systematically denied. Artist managers need new ways to help artists build genuinely direct connections with their audiences so that artists can build more sustainable businesses, because: 'Anyone who works in the music industry will be familiar with the underlying sense of inequality' (Connolly, 2021b).

As I previously outlined in Chapter 3, the circular career development model generates a perception that direct connections between an artist and their audience are being facilitated by multi-sided platforms such as Spotify, Apple Music, Facebook, Instagram and TikTok. However, what is actually happening is that artists have indirect relationships with their audience through these types of platforms because the connections are occurring within these platform's walled fortresses. Artists cannot take their fan data outside of these fortresses because they are surrounded by moats. Within the context of the creator economy, Connolly (2021b) argued that artists can strategically work toward building genuinely direct relationships with their audiences that involve them retaining their audience data through the services provided by Circle, Memberful, Substack, Ghost and others.[4] According to Connolly, these services enable artists to build genuinely direct relationships with audiences.

Further, the externalisation of risk onto music artists and managers through the advent of label services deals and the like, as discussed in Chapter 4, means that streamlined and stripped back record labels are providing fewer services than they did in the past in exchange for a licence of the artist's copyright, or an assignment of it for the life of copyright. If early-stage financing is the main reason left for artists to do these types of agreements, Connolly (2021b) argued that there is a clear alternative for this: equity financing. For him, more early-stage financing options for artists may help to further shift the power dynamics discussed throughout this book in the artists' favour. This in turn would help music artist managers' businesses become more sustainable. Connolly cited the following early-stage equity financing entities: Slow Ventures (n.d.), Creative Juice (2023) and Atelier Ventures (2020).

Different methods for raising early-stage financing for music artists could be modelled on the approach taken by many tech start-ups, whereby investors provide funding in exchange for equity (shares) in the company that is established. The difference between this and past deal making in the record business is that the investor invests without requiring a transfer of the copyright to them or a licence: 'If Blackbird meets a start-up whose IP has been licensed to some other entity, we cannot invest in them' (Connolly, 2021b). What is interesting about Connolly's discussion of this model is the fluidity it could bring to the ways in which artists can incentivise the people they need to help them build their businesses. For Connolly, this fluidity could be maximised if a band, for example, formed a company for each album or collection of songs released, with the band members being the founders and initial shareholders in the project. Then instead of licensing the copyright or assigning it to another entity, the band could sell equity (shares in the company) to others who would then be incentivised to increase the value of the project.

A music artist manager could be given equity; and likewise a booking agent, a publicist, etc. could be given equity; and a record label, or even a collection of labels, could buy equity. The music artist manager's role would then involve coordinating and persuading these shareholders to work together to increase the value of the album project. In my earlier work (Morrow,

2018), I applied the principles of agile project management to artist management, and what Connolly (2021b) is proposing would bring more agility to the music business. Bands, for example, could more effectively operate on a project-by-project basis like the dance, film and theatrical industries do. Doing so would help musicians to get into a state of what social psychologist Keith Sawyer (2003, 2017) termed group flow more often. Group flow involves the highly enjoyable psychological state that teams or groups get into when they are performing at their peak. While some familiarity with each other is required, the novelty and discovery that comes with working with new people is key to this state, and therefore this theory can explain the relatively short lifespan of rewarding collaboration in the arts. An extreme example is improv theatre: 'Chicago improv ensembles rarely continue performing together for more than three months, and many shows last for much less than that before the members move on and form new combinations with actors likewise freed from other mature groups' (Sawyer, as cited in Morrow, 2018, p. 5). The film industry is another example. Investors come together to invest in a single film project in anticipation of getting returns from the takings. The production time of a film and a music album are also similar.

For Connolly (2021b), the advantages of an equity financing approach in the field of popular music are similar because it would involve 'liquidity in creative works'. Shares in the company that controls the underlying assets (copyrights) could more easily be bought and sold; 'band members are not so locked in'. If the band members' equity is held in the project, not the band, this could facilitate more collaboration and creativity, and if shares in such creative works could be bought and sold, then each contributor to an artist's career could be better incentivised. This would encourage them by creating the opportunity to build long-term wealth through the ownership of assets which are shares in the companies set up for different albums, not the copyright. Through this model, fans would potentially also be able to buy shares in albums or projects through a type of crowdfunding, thus enabling artists to build very direct relationships with them. Linking this to the post-term commission discussion earlier, and Jake Udell's (2019) argument that post-term participation in revenue should include new recordings that are produced after termination, if the manager had equity in the company set up for the album, then they would not participate in the revenue from new recordings or projects unless they are also given equity in subsequent companies that are established.

Another idea circling around that could arguably also facilitate more fluidity in deal making for artists was put forth by Giblin (2018) and Giblin and Doctorow (2022). This idea involves enshrining in law an automatic reversion of copyright to the artist 25 years after transfer. Obviously, in contrast to Connolly's (2021b) proposal earlier, Giblin's (2018) proposal would involve legislative change relating to copyright generally through a process of completely reimagining what it could look like. Giblin (2018) and Giblin and Doctorow (2022) chose 25 years because, according to them, this would maintain incentives for record labels, etc. to make the initial investment, then after 25 years the artist could re-exploit their recordings in new ways with new partners, or they could agree to new terms with their original investors. While under existing copyright law, artists can licence their copyright for 25 years, then have it revert to them as a term of the contract. Giblin (2018) and Giblin and Doctorow (2022) argued that the power the dominant corporations have makes this extremely difficult to achieve. This is why they proposed changing the law to make such a reversion automatic. This would also mean that major record labels would no longer have the monopoly-building advantage stemming from their deep catalogue. In this way, more artist-friendly business models could emerge (see Giblin & Doctorow, 2022, pp. 190–195 for more on this).

Rather than transferring the copyright to them for the full period of copyright in perpetuity, what Giblin (2018) and Giblin and Doctorow (2022) proposed would make shorter-term control of copyright automatic because ownership of copyright would revert to the creator after 25 years so that the creator can benefit from it again. This would involve a radical change in current copyright law given that, for example, the full period of copyright in the US and Australia is for the life of the author plus 70 years, and in Canada and New Zealand it is life of the author plus 50 years (Giblin & Doctorow, 2022, p. 193). The first modern copyright law was the 1710 Statute of Anne, and this gave the authors exclusive rights for 14 years, and then if they were alive after this period, they were granted exclusive rights for another 14 years (p. 182).

The opportunity for artists to be able to sell copyright more than once is important. For example, when I was co-managing Australian band Boy & Bear through their first EP and then album cycle (2008–11), my co-manager Rowan Brand and I, along with the band and the band's lawyer Julian Hewitt, managed to procure a licence agreement for Australia and New Zealand only from Universal Music Australia (UMA). We were only able to do this due to an extraordinary amount of interest from other major labels at the time, such as EMI, which gave the band leverage. This interest was triggered by youth radio station Triple J's championing of the band. Looking back, it was quite a remarkable achievement.[5] However, it was only possible because EMI was a separate major label at the time, and their willingness to do such a deal was key to UMA agreeing to do it. Now that UMA owns EMI, this ability to leverage a better deal for the artist due to competition between major labels is lessened. For Boy & Bear, the deal we made means that the rights to the recordings made during the term of their agreement with UMA will revert to them ten years after the release of the last album commitment. The period was therefore relative to whether UMA proceeded with all the four album options in the agreement and when these options were exercised, as opposed to the set 25 years Giblin (2018) proposed. This band, however, will get the rights back, and they will be able to re-exploit them. What Giblin (2018) and Giblin and Doctorow (2022) are proposing would make this type of agreement the default setting. But it would involve changing copyright law, and therefore what Connolly (2021b) proposed earlier could be realised sooner.

The less work model

A challenge for music artist managers who attempt to negotiate for more equitable ways to distribute the value that is collected from the creation of music is, according to one Australian artist manager who participated in this study,

> this idea that's been pushed onto artists for many years by various different people, saying that 'You don't have to worry about what's going on over here with the numbers side of things or the structure side of things. You just focus on your music, we'll take care of everything else.'
>
> (Interview 5)

The culture within the music business has been shaped by the most powerful corporations within it because of the economic power they have. The dominant players have shaped it in a way that makes it easier to co-opt most of the economic value artists generate by way of the contracts outlined throughout this book. Artists not worrying about what is going on contributes to this. This has no doubt suited the interests of some unscrupulous managers too, whose efforts have in part led to the problematic perception of the permanence of industry norms that was outlined in Chapter 3. However, the fact that big tech and big content companies have continued to be able to capture this creative labour market, with major labels and publishers building bigger and bigger monopolies, means that artists must realise that they have a key role in establishing more equitable ways to distribute *their* value and do some of the heavy lifting required to better their situation. The Australian artist manager cited earlier continued: 'Artists have to take on the knowledge, education and responsibility of their business. And that won't even put a manager out of their job. It will just make a manager's job easier' (Interview 5).

A key solution to many of the problems outlined in this book, therefore, is cultural change to persuade artists to do more of the work. The type of management agreements outlined in Chapter 1 are not sustainable because of the amount of work that managers must do. Rather than carving out more of the artist's revenue by way of a higher percentage that is closer to gross revenue than net revenue, the manager cited earlier argued that, because artists often do not have any more to give,

> it's actually about carving out the work within that job of management that you can't do, literally, because there are not enough hours in the day for you to do it. And potentially still sticking with that 20% for now . . . the

artist actually culturally needs to take on more responsibility for themselves as a business. There are so many small business grants out there, tax incentives, rebates, etc., and artists don't even think they're for them, because they don't even consider that they are a business. And if you look at other creative industries, in particular, the fashion industry, the creative leaders in those industries are expected to be not just the creative leads, but the bosses, they create brands that create partnerships, they know how to manage people, they understand what their business is, they have to understand the financials of their business, they have to be the CEO of their own business and tell other people what to do.

(Interview 5)

In contrast to this, in the experience of another Australian artist manager,

Artists often don't engage in the financial conversations, or take the time to truly understand the details of a given tour, or their business as a whole. Few managers have a full grasp of this business side either I suspect, but there is a real issue with artists and managers not having transparent conversations about the business, and artists not owning their role as a business owner. So often the conversations are also just happening quickly on a phone call, and nothing is in writing.

(Interview 8)

This reluctance to take on full responsibility among some artists can not only cause managers stress but, depending on the terms of their management agreement, can introduce the risk that managers could be deemed to have breached their management agreement:

Even legally, I have heard anecdotally that some lawyers are pushing against post-term commissions because an artist might not have approved certain business expenses which are part of the day to day running of the business and touring. There does need to be more established practice on this for both parties' sakes, but if artists are not engaging in the business and the established dynamic is that the manager runs everything, it doesn't seem right that it gets raised as an issue only when a contract ends, like 'No, you don't get post-terms because you didn't get permission for these flights'.

(Interview 8)

A change in the culture of the music business, as in 'the way we do things around here' (Bower 1966, as cited in Saintilan & Schreiber, 2018, p. 213), is needed. While artists may feel that it is part of their role to be disinterested in their own business, one solution to some of the issues outlined in this book is for managers to do less work for the same amount of remuneration, and artificial intelligence (AI) may help in this regard too.

Artificial intelligence

During the timeframe for researching and writing this book, awareness of the potential impact of artificial intelligence (AI) exploded. One Australian artist manager who participated, Keith Welsh, pointed out:

> We're about to see another huge, huge problem with the whole AI-generated world. And I don't think that artist managers, collectively, have a view about how they're going to talk to government about that and how they're going to talk to their copyright partners about that in order to get some form of framework to actually stop there being a flood of, you know, [Australian music artist] Flume tracks which Flume didn't actually make. And that applies to all Australian artists who have any kind of success. What are we going to do with Spotify and what are we going to do with Apple Music to stop those things actually having any distribution? So that, to me, is a huge thing for AAM to do. So, I think they need to, yes, reinforce all the social stuff they've done over the last few years, but they've really got to turn back into a quite aggressive commercial organisation, because there's a lot about the money now which is about to change radically.
>
> (Interview 11)

Following this interview with Welsh in early 2023, at SXSW Festival Sydney in late 2023 I met with Annabella Coldrick, who is the chief executive of the Music Managers Forum (MMF) in the United Kingdom. Coldrick gave me a copy of *The music manager's (interim) guide to AI* (Cooke & Taylor, 2023), which the MMF published in September 2023. The guide outlines the threats and opportunities presented by generative AI. The MMF called it an interim guide because the technology and associated regulatory frameworks were at the time evolving so quickly that it was envisaged that the guide would need regular updating.

AI has the potential both to increase and to decrease music artist managers' workloads. For a start, understanding the ways in which AI tools can enhance and assist both artists' and managers' businesses involves a new and demanding cognitive load. For example, as the MMF guide advises, the requirement for artists and managers to be aware of what rights they are granting when they use AI tools is important. Further, the challenges of understanding how artists who are already subject to agreements with record labels and song publishers can use AI in their creative processes increases the manager's workload because there is a need to revisit the terms of the artist's extant agreements. In addition, understanding how to factor AI into the negotiation of new deals with labels, distributors or publishers also increases the manager's workload; publicity, image and personality rights have come to the fore because artists and managers need to be particularly careful in granting any rights beyond copyright to business partners (see Cooke & Taylor, 2023, p. 12 for more on this). Further, music artist managers have a key role to play in holding rights holders to account regarding the transparency of their AI deals and revenues, and this is the role that Keith Welsh was asking the AAM to play in the interview for this project cited earlier. At the end of their guide, the MMF provided an AI checklist for managers that included the following items:

- Music makers and managers should be aware of what rights they are granting when they use AI tools.
- AI companies and rights holders must seek explicit music-maker consent.
- Rights holders should involve music makers and managers in the development of AI business models (Cooke & Taylor, 2023, p. 22).

Yet, for all the additional work navigating the AI frontier requires of managers, the technology presents managers with opportunities for building on the 'less work model' outlined earlier.

In November 2023, I met Dr Martin Clancy at the Kristiansand Roundtable Conference in Norway. Clancy's contributed volume *Artificial intelligence and music ecosystem* (Clancy, 2022a) highlights the opportunities and rewards associated with the application of AI in both the field of music and the broader creative arts. Over dinner, Clancy put a convincing argument that AI will lessen managers' workloads.

Clancy noted that there are many ways in which artists and managers are using or can use AI—including generative AI—as part of both the music-making process and the processes associated with managing, promoting and disseminating the music that is produced. His argument aligned with that put in the MMF guide—that managers can use it 'to help generate and distribute marketing content; to better manage rights and royalties; to handle basic legal and admin tasks; and to more effectively run music businesses' (Cooke & Taylor, 2023, p. 6). The specific areas highlighted in the MMF guide included song writing and recording; production and mastering; marketing and visual content; data management; document creation; translation; and initial research and idea generation. The AI tools that the MMF guide recommended managers consider are ChatGPT, Bard, Grammarly, Otter.ai, DreamStudio from Stability AI, Midjourney, Kaiber, Gen 1/Gen 2 by Runway, Voice-Swap and Elevenlabs (p. 7).

As I outlined in Chapter 2, music artist managers are taking the lead in helping to bring the artists' creative visions to life through social media. This has dramatically increased managers' workloads because more visual content needs to be generated and disseminated around the release of their artist's music. As I noted in my earlier work concerning design culture in the music business,

the shift of audience attention away from television to streaming services such as Netflix and toward social media has led to a fracturing of what was previously more focused and singular content such as a single advertisement on television or a lone music video.

(Morrow, 2020, p. 111)

At the time I was researching and writing this 2020 book, this shift had led to the rise of package deals between music video directors and musicians. For example, the package may include

> a 'half documentary' that could work as a singular piece of content but that could also be split into six episodes that were 5 minutes in length each. This content was drip fed over the course of the release. . . . The collection of episodes was then hosted online as one single documentary after the release. . . . The package deal also included the production of 2 x 1-minute trailers/teasers, 4 x 30-second social media snippets, 4 x 15-second social media snippets and 1 x full music video for the new single. . . . This music video was used promotionally with the documentary and the social media snippet footage. . . . This fracturing of content into such package deals is a reaction to the fracturing of audiences' attention due to social media.

(p. 111)

AI tools can assist with the huge volume of work that such packages of audio-visual content involve. Some of the services mentioned earlier, such as DreamStudio from Stability AI and Midjourney, are prompt-based image generation tools, while Kaiber and Gen 1/Gen 2 by Runway both use AI to generate videos. Another service that promises to lessen the workload for artists, managers and visual content creators is Blurb. Blurb promises to

> turn one track into countless videos. . . . We scale content creation for music companies. On-brand video that drives streams, fills arenas, markets merch and cultivates fanbases—all on autopilot. . . . We're putting the most foundational pieces of creative on autopilot, so that your teams can focus on strategic priorities.

(Blurb, 2024)

Blurb promises to power scalable content creation by functioning as the equivalent of a record company's art department, but one that is not limited to working on one project at a time.

While such use of AI-based services to generate images and video will theoretically reduce managers' workloads, Clancy's (2022b) argument is even more significant. Clancy argued that ethical use of AI in the music business has the potential to address the value gap; this has profound implications for managers' role in advocating for music artists, and, in doing so, they can also advocate for themselves.

According to Clancy (2022b), music artist managers have an opportunity here to show leadership regarding the ethical use of AI. As I outlined in Chapter 4 of this book, major record labels' deep catalogues, and the fact that they invested in services such as Spotify in the first instance, means that the revenues from such services are directed towards major stars and major record labels rather than benefiting all musicians in the same manner (Eriksson et al., 2019, p. 3). Spotify's business model has, therefore, perpetuated a pre-existing value gap in the chain of income earned through music streaming. Although, as I will outline later, Spotify themselves argued that this is changing, Dahrooge (2021) articulated this value gap in the following way: '[On] average, Spotify pays US$ 0.00437 per average play, meaning that an artist will need roughly 336,842 total plays to earn US$ 1,472. While in comparison, Spotify has an annual revenue of US$ 4.99 billion through its paid subscribers' (Dahrooge, 2021, pp. 212–213).

In response to the claims of Eriksson et al. (2019, p. 3) and others that Spotify's business model does not depart from the winner-take-all models of traditional media industries, in 2021 Spotify launched Loud & Clear. Spotify designed Loud & Clear to break down their royalty system and overall process for musicians. Loud & Clear involves Spotify publishing on their website what they claim are the ten key points concerning the economics of music streaming based on Spotify's 2021 royalty data. For instance, they claim that over 1,000 artists generated USD 1 million on Spotify in 2021; that 500,000 artists generated USD 10,000 from their platform; that the top 50 music artists in the world were favoured twice as much in the CD era as compared to now; and that the music industries in emerging markets are benefiting more from streaming revenue than they did during previous eras from other formats (Spotify, 2022).

As I have argued throughout this book, a key role of the music artist manager is to help music artists to reduce the value gap that exists between them and services such as Spotify. While through Loud & Clear Spotify themselves argued that this gap is reducing, for Clancy (2022b), the posthumanist thought engendered by AI can potentially accelerate the closing of this gap:

The inclusion of posthumanist thought can actively contribute towards a significant reimagining of the concept of 'human-centred values'. . . . This realignment of values turns into a legal question: how do human and non-human actors—including the development of AI—become interlinked in a sustainable and equitable music ecosystem? In comparison to humanism and transhumanism, posthumanism offers the third philosophical approach beyond the dominating binary positions of either a dystopian vision, where AI technologies embark on a hostile takeover (robots stealing jobs), or the alternate utopian model in which AI technologies are beneficial to human spheres of existence (as helpers, companions, and care workers).

(p. 173)

It is through the third philosophical approach offered by posthumanism that the term 'music ecosystem' comes to life for Clancy; Clancy embraces elements of actor-network theory to consider human and nonhuman (AI) 'member organisms' as stakeholders of the global music community, including the commercial music industries.

Clancy cited Paul McCartney, who argued that 'the value gap jeopardises the music ecosystem [its narrowing will] . . . help assure a sustainable future for the music ecosystem and its creators' (McCartney, as cited in Clancy, 2022b, p. 178). For Clancy, there is an opportunity here for this new interaction between human and nonhuman (AI) 'member organisms' of the music ecosystem to engender ethical considerations of issues such as music copyright that can usher in a more sustainable and fairer environment for music creation and commercialisation. His theoretical model underpins 'an ethical AI "fair trade" mark to support a fair and sustainable music ecosystem' (p. 2).

To realise this ambition of establishing an ethical AI 'fair trade' mark, Clancy developed an initiative entitled AI:OK (2023). The AI:OK logo is designed to represent 'a secure and trustworthy certification for approved music, products and services within the music ecosystem in the era of Generative AI and future technologies' (AI:OK, 2023). The problem that AI:OK addresses is that presently consumers and stakeholders are usually unaware which music content is AI generated. Further, for AI:OK, knowing whether AI was used is not enough; the logo also needs to signal whether AI is encouraging human creativity or replacing it:

> The AI:OK logo benefits the industry by defining and managing sustainable AI use standards and fostering trust among consumers and creators. It reassures stakeholders regarding the equitable sourcing and creation of AI-driven services and products while providing creators with a mark of quality and compliance that enhances their artistic and commercial credibility.
>
> (AI:OK, 2023)

The goals of AI:OK align with those of the AAM; both have an interest in creating a more sustainable playing field for music artists and music industry stakeholders, including music artist managers. Therefore AI:OK is an initiative that music artist managers can potentially use in the age of generative AI to help close the value gap. The AI:OK initiative has the potential to help address many of the issues outlined in this book.

Conclusion

Music artist managers are part of a larger cultural ecosystem. A theme emerged across the various ideas for new models for music artist manager retention that I uncovered through this research. This theme is the need for more decentralisation in the music business. If realised, the models outlined in this chapter would help develop a healthier, stronger and more independent manager community, and this would in turn lead to a more diverse and sustainable cultural ecosystem overall, one with more players and less power in the hands of a few.

Music artists and their managers are engaged in an ever-bigger David-versus-Goliath battle. The power of major labels has grown, and it is in this context that a strong and independent artist manager community can help to lobby for initiatives such as minimum wages for creative labour that would give artists an 'inalienable right to appropriate and proportionate pay for the use of their work' (Giblin & Doctorow, 2022, p. 214). For example, there is a new EU law that grants creators residual remuneration rights (p. 214). Such legal rights enable artists to avoid rights buyouts such as those imposed by Netflix (p. 215) on some documentary film composers by making 'back-end' payments mandatory.

Many of the ideas covered in this chapter concern the general principle of establishing better enduring entitlements for music artist managers. Girgis's (2019) argument that management agreements could be amended to reflect record producer agreements; the various arguments that post-term commission structures should be lengthened and could include participation in perpetuity; and Connolly's (2021b) equity finance model all involve managers in various ways having more of a stake in the 'back end' by way of enduring entitlements.

Realisation of the models presented in this chapter is crucial for the larger cultural ecosystem that the work of artists feeds. In principle, music artists' and music artist managers' interests are meant to co-align. It is problematic that at present managers typically do not have a meaningful stake in the back end because they are important stakeholders who, alongside the artist, have an interest in conducting negotiations with the ever-growing and monopolising multinational corporations mentioned in this chapter. Artists' and managers' interests need to truly co-align when it comes to the back end. While residual remuneration rights can be established for artists in law, better incentivising managers is one of the keys to the collective efforts required to establish such laws. If realised, the models outlined in this chapter could lead to more fluidity, liquidity and agility in the music business while also decentralising power within the larger cultural ecosystem.

Perhaps the most significant opportunity here is for music artist managers to show leadership regarding the ethical use of AI to help close the value gap. Clancy's (2022b; AI:OK, 2023) work is potentially important here. Rather than presenting a dystopian vision of the future that involves a hostile takeover of the music business by robots who steal music artists' jobs and other music industry stakeholders' positions, Clancy's (2022a) remarkably optimistic book and initiative AI:OK highlights the opportunities and rewards associated with the application of AI in the field of music. Artists and managers are in some of the best positions to harness these opportunities.

Notes

1 Giblin and Doctorow (2022) argued that the way recoupment is structured in recording agreements is a peculiar feature for agreements within the broader context of creative labour markets.
2 A Judas goat is a goat that is trained to assist in the herding of animals such as sheep or cattle. The Judas goat leads the other animals to a destination that the farmer dictates, including to a slaughterhouse. While the other animals such as sheep are slaughtered, the life of the Judas goat is spared (Morrow, 2018, p. 110).
3 Live Nation's rival TEG owns Australia's largest ticketing agency Ticketek (Sainsbury, 2022), which provides it with a similar opportunity to poach artists from independent managers and live booking agents.
4 For an overview of the creator economy Connolly (2021b) recommends Yuan and Constine (2020).
5 We signed the band to the Island Records imprint of UMA after an intense bidding process that enabled us to secure a licence agreement for Australia and New Zealand only. We then signed the band's publishing to Sony/ATV for the world and went about trying to sign the band directly to a label in the US or UK. This led to tension with UMA. Further, a major label typically wants to sell one million records in one year and then move onto the next big artist, but the band and us as their managers wanted to sell 100,000 for 10 years and have sustainable careers. This also led to tension between UMA and the band/us. Despite our deal making in the US falling over, the band went on to win five Australian Recording Industry Association awards in 2011 due to the band's, Island/UMA's and our efforts and I'm pleased to see that 14 years on the band are achieving relatively high streaming numbers and selling out shows worldwide and ultimately are sustaining their career(s) now as independent artists.

References

AI:OK. (2023). *About*. https://ai-ok.org/
Atelier Ventures. (2020). *Atelier*. www.atelierventures.co/
Blurb. (2024). *Blurb*. https://blurb.fm/
Clancy, M. (Ed.). (2022a). *Artificial intelligence and music ecosystem*. Focal Press. https://doi.org/10.4324/9780429356797
Clancy, M. (2022b). Philosophy: Amor Fati: A theoretical model of the music ecosystem. In M. Clancy (Ed.), *Artificial intelligence and music ecosystem* (pp. 165–181). Focal Press. https://doi.org/10.4324/9780429356797
Connolly, J. (2021a, April 12). How the music industry stifles creativity and denies artists their agency. *Meaning Making*. https://joelconnolly.substack.com/p/how-the-music-industry-stifles-creativity
Connolly, J. (2021b, June 8). Decentralising the music industry: Ideas on equity financing, the creator economy, bitcoin. *Meaning making*. https://joelconnolly.substack.com/p/decentralising-the-music-industry
Cooke, C., & Taylor, S. (2023). *The music manager's (interim) guide to AI*. Music Managers' Forum, UK.

Creative Juice. (2023). *Banking for creators.* www.getjuice.com/

Dahrooge, J. J. (2021). *The real Slim Shady: How Spotify and other music streaming services are taking advantage of the loopholes within the Music Modernization Act.* https://law-journals-books.vlex.com/vid/the-real-slim-shady-870462443

Eriksson, M., Fleischer, R., Johansson, A., Snickars, P., & Vonderau, P. (2019). *Spotify teardown: Inside the black box of streaming music.* MIT Press.

Giblin, R. (2018). A new copyright bargain? Reclaiming lost culture and getting authors paid. *Columbia Journal of Law & the Arts, 41*(3), Article 3. https://doi.org/10.7916/jla.v41i3.2019

Giblin, R., & Doctorow, C. (2022). *Chokepoint capitalism: How big tech and big content captured creative labor markets and how we'll win them back.* Scribe Publications.

Girgis, L. (2019, March 12). It's time artist managers got paid properly. *The Music Network.* https://themusicnetwork.com/its-time-artist-managers-got-paid-properly/

Ingham, T. (2020, June 8). Labels could start helping Black artists by adjusting old record deals. *Rolling Stone.* www.rollingstone.com/pro/features/music-black-artists-old-record-deals-1011447/

Morrow, G. (2006). *Managerial creativity: A study of artist management practices in the Australian popular music industry* [Doctoral thesis, Macquarie University]. Figshare. https://figshare.mq.edu.au/articles/thesis/Managerial_creativity_a_study_of_artist_management_practices_in_the_Australian_popular_music_industry/19427489

Morrow, G. (2018). *Artist management: Agility in the creative and cultural industries.* Routledge.

Morrow, G. (2020). *Designing the music business: Design culture, music video and virtual reality.* Springer International Publishing. https://doi.org/10.1007/978-3-030-48114-8

Philips, C. (2002, February 26). Auditors put new spin on revolt over royalties. *Los Angeles Times.* www.latimes.com/archives/la-xpm-2002-feb-26-mn-29955-story.html

Sainsbury, M. (2022, October 28). The overseas giants swallowing Australia's live music industry. *The Sydney Morning Herald.* www.smh.com.au/culture/music/the-overseas-giants-swallowing-australia-s-live-music-industry-20221026-p5bt01.html

Saintilan, P., & Schreiber, D. (2018). *Managing organizations in the creative economy: Organizational behaviour for the cultural sector.* Routledge.

Sawyer, K. (2017). *Group genius: The creative power of collaboration.* Hachette UK.

Sawyer, R. K. (2003). *Group creativity: Music, theater, collaboration.* Psychology Press.

Slow Ventures. (n.d.). *Slow ventures.* https://slow.co

Spotify. (2022, March 24). *Spotify's top 10 takeaways on the economics of music streaming and 2021 royalty data.* https://newsroom.spotify.com/2022-03-24/spotifys-top-10-takeaways-on-the-economics-of-music-streaming-and-2021-royalty-data/

Tschmuck, P. (2017). *The economics of music*. Agenda Publishing. https://doi.org/10.2307/j.ctv5cg90z

Udell, J. (2019, March 25). TH3RD BRAIN's Jake Udell on management commissions. *The Music Network*. https://themusicnetwork.com/jake-udell-on-management-commissions/

Yuan, Y., & Constine, J. (2020, November 29). SignalFire's creator economy market map. *Signal Fire*. www.signalfire.com/blog/creator-economy

Conclusion

The significance of this book is that it provides transparency. Music artist managers in Australia often work as isolated sole traders or through relatively small companies and firms. Further, in Australia, while music artists can join the Media, Entertainment and Arts Alliance, there is no music specific artist collective that is equivalent to the Featured Artists' Coalition in the UK through which the different perspectives and interests of others can be shared. This lack of transparency is problematic because it perpetuates issues such as the illusion of permanence regarding management agreement terms that are unsustainable for managers. This then works against artists because the people with the knowledge of the business, who could directly help them, leave the business, or they move sideways within the music business and away from artist management as fast as they can.

This is a problem because certain parts of this business are mind-numbingly complex. Music licensing, for example, is notoriously complex, and, whether this is intentional or not, major record and song publishing companies who own most of the commercial content benefit from this opacity. The biggest beneficiaries of the existing way of doing things in the field of music artist management, therefore, are not artists, but the most powerful record labels, song publishers and live music promoters. The changes and recommendations put forth in this book concerning the field of music artist management have the potential to curtail the power of these dominant stakeholders by helping to establish a more diverse and sustainable cultural ecosystem overall.

This book has shone a spotlight on what is going on in the field of music artist management in Australia, and this type of transparency is key for creating the countervailing power that music artist managers need to put pressure on multinational companies to do the right thing by artists. By zooming out and providing a bird's-eye view, the research contained in this book has the potential to help transform the atomised exploitation of both artists and managers into powerful solidarity. The AAM has a key role to play in the collective action that is required to help rebalance power relations between music artists and the most powerful companies in the music business, companies that are now much bigger than they used to be.

DOI: 10.4324/9781003388005-7

Just as the safety briefing on an aeroplane emphasises the importance of putting one's own oxygen mask on first before helping others, this metaphor applies to music artist managers. Music artist managers are advocates for artists, but they need more oxygen. The issues discussed in this book are urgent because the sooner more oxygen starts flowing, the sooner managers, and more specifically the collective of managers that the AAM represents, can better advocate for artists.

The oxygen needs to flow through a needs-supportive framework that includes both non-financial and financial rewards. The research problem this book explored was: to what extent is it possible for managers to do good, enjoyable and fulfilling work in music artist management? By answering this question, I sought to emphasise the quality of the subjective experience of music artist managers. What kinds of experiences does the role of artist management in the music industries offer? Can a framework for needs-supportive artist-to-manager leadership address some of the problems managers are experiencing?

Music artist management can be good work through meeting the three universal psychological needs that are essential for optimal development and functioning: autonomy, relatedness and competence. Out of these three needs, relatedness is key and is the starting point. As outlined in Chapter 2, the participants articulated a special type of relatedness that involves artistic creativity. This need is met when the role provides managers with a sense of belonging to a broader community, including a strong connection to artists. Through being so close to the artistically creative process, managers feel meaningfully involved with the broader social world. This broader relatedness occurs particularly through the way in which artists in turn connect with their audiences, and the way the music that managers help to create can incite change within this broader social world. Because the psychological need for relatedness is the key motivation here, and this partly involves a strong connection to the artist, if artists were to provide positive feedback and choice through their leadership of managers, this could help to support this need.

This book has focused on the motivation of music artist managers themselves. While the research findings did indicate that managers are primarily intrinsically motivated through the way their psychological need for autonomy, relatedness and competence are met, financial rewards are important too. For music artist managers, financial reward management and non-financial reward management are interrelated. A financial reward structure that makes managers relatively disposable influences how they are treated, how they feel and how motivated they are. To this end, both better financial and non-financial reward management, total reward theory, could be utilised. More progressive artist management agreements or shareholder agreements that provide equity in the musicians' businesses that managers help to create could better incentivise music artist managers. Such agreements, stemming from the new models for music artist manager retention that were outlined in Chapter 5, could better enable artists to motivate, rather than negatively lead, their managers. This is because such agreements would change the power dynamic between the artist and the manager. This could help to address some of the problematic artist behaviour that was disclosed in the survey, interviews and focus groups.

There are several areas for further research. In 2023, the Australian federal Labor government launched 'Australia's Cultural Policy for the next five years. Revive: A place for every story, a story for every place'. Pillar 3 of this national cultural policy is entitled 'Centrality of the Artist: Supporting the artist as worker and celebrating artists as creators' (Office for the Arts, 2023). The role of music artist managers, including their artist advocacy, aligns with this pillar. Further research is needed into the links between the actions stemming from this pillar and some of the issues uncovered in this book, such as artist-to-manager bullying, and the ideas presented concerning the automatic reversion of copyright to the creator 25 years after any licence or assignment of it.

In the consultation period prior to the launch of this policy, the Association of Artist Managers developed its National Cultural Policy Submission (AAM, 2022) and presented it to the Australian government. Further research is needed into the issues and solutions that it contained. The core issues identified were lack of First Nations managers, female manager retention and lack of representation and support. The solutions were entitled Core Funding for the AAM; Offset staff for SME [Small and Medium Enterprises] Employers via a Paid Internship Program; and Funding that Allows for Investment in Managers and their Businesses Directly. Of these solutions, the one entitled 'Offset staff for SME Employers via a Paid Internship Program', according to the AAM, would 'create affordable access for every Australian to the industry and relieve burnt out managers of their workloads. It would also create a safety net for female managers looking to take maternity leave' (AAM, 2022). The issue of parental leave, or lack thereof, is a significant one for music artist managers. It is therefore in itself also an area for further research. Research into the extent to which the establishment of larger management firms in Australia, such as Melbourne-based companies Unified Music Group and Lemon Tree Music, has led to the provision of better parental leave options for music artist managers would also be worthwhile to consider in further research.

References

Association of Artist Managers (AAM). (2022). *National cultural policy submission*. www.aam.org.au/cps2022

Office for the Arts. (2023). *National cultural policy—Revive: A place for every story, a story for every place*. www.arts.gov.au/publications/national-cultural-policy-revive-place-every-story-story-every-place

Index